24 MONTHS TO FREEDOM

24 MONTHS TO FREEDOM

How modern law firms
use smarter staffing solutions to
fast track their way to success

BRETT TREMBLY

Unstoppable CEO Press

Brett Trembly
brett@getstaffedup.com
www.24monthstofreedom.com

24 Months to Freedom, Brett Trembly —1st ed. ISBN 978-1-955242-43-1

CONTENTS

Introduction

Are you running your law firm, or is your law firm running you?

You likely started your own firm because you either wanted to help people, had a vision for a different type of firm, or wanted to do it your own way, or some combination of all three. You had energy and passion and were ready to take on the world. So you made the leap and hung your own shingle, but much isn't going as planned.

If you're like me more than 10 years ago, instead of creating a business, you gave yourself a difficult job, and one with little pay and lots of overtime, to boot. You're overworked, and the hours you put in aren't reflected when you count your revenue. You spend more time doing tedious admin tasks than producing meaningful work for your clients. Weeks pass at a time, and you figure it'll get better, eventually. You work hard, but you're stuck on the hamster wheel. Always moving, always ending up right back where you started.

This isn't the life you dreamed of when you set out to build your own practice. You're still on your own and have no idea how you can hire anyone. Or, maybe you've had some initial success and have hired an employee or two, but you're stuck. With every hire, overhead growth keeps up with revenue, and it makes you wonder, what's the point?

Here's the problem: as smart as attorneys are, we were never taught how to run a business. We know how to win a case, but we have no idea how to get clients, build a team, organize our finances, and ultimately grow our firms. Regardless of how big of a law firm we each desire to build, one thing we can probably all agree on is that we became lawyers to live a happy, comfortable lifestyle, and this requires a business which doesn't depend on us 24/7.

You know there's a better way and that you'll need a team to get there, but you don't know where to start. I'm here to help. In this book, I lay out a 24-month plan to take you from feeling stuck and helpless to living what I call the *Liberated Lawyer Lifestyle.* As you move through these 24 months, you'll take some smart and calculated risks (breathe deep, there is no growth without action), your revenue will grow, and you'll work fewer hours.

What's the secret to reaching the *Liberated Lawyer Lifestyle*? Before you can earn more money, you have to buy back your time. By building your firm in a smarter and more cost-efficient way with virtual staff, you'll engage more clients, produce more work, and grow your firm… to the point that you run the business and it no longer runs you.

Does the phrase, "hire a team," scare you? I know what many of you are thinking, *I can't afford to hire right now.*

Yes, you can. With the rise of remote work, you can hire a team from all over the world comprised of the best and brightest English-speaking talent in the international workforce. And because the U.S. dollar goes so much farther in most countries, you can afford to hire extremely qualified workers for a fraction of what similar talent and experience costs domestically.

I've helped countless law firm owners recruit virtual team members, and I've experienced how this model transforms businesses. Your practice can evolve from a chaotic operation wholly dependent on you, into a machine that you steer, direct and improve as you see fit. Yes, your business can be a "thing" that runs separately from you, and you should strive to perceive it that way.

It only takes 24 months to *prudently* build a team large enough to start giving you freedom, and you'll begin noticing results with your very first hire.

Will you be lounging on beaches and never having to lift a finger for your firm again 24 months from now? I hope so, but it's doubtful. While living the high life may come later, the real life you dreamed of when you set out to build a practice – the one in which you have the financial and time freedom to make decisions based on your wants, needs and values – is not only possible, it's probable when you follow the game plan in this book.

Stepping off the hamster wheel is closer than you think. You don't have to stay stuck where you are now. Let me show you the way out...

PART I

Being Honest with the One Person Who Really Matters - Yourself

CHAPTER ONE

The Reality of Running a Small Law Firm Today

If you run a small law firm, I'm familiar with what the substantial part of your work day looks like. You most likely start your day by reading and answering emails. There are a few items on your calendar in the morning, but you don't always get to them. A couple calls interrupt you and you have to shift gears to put out some fires. Maybe you have an employee or two, and they're full of questions and need your attention. Midday hits, and you haven't done any legal work yet, despite this always being your top priority. You run out to a networking lunch, and when you come back, you're tired. It's finally time to get to the work that's been eluding you all day, but more interruptions happen. You then remember to post an update on social media late in the day, but get sucked into scrolling.

Before you know it, the time you swore you'd stop work is upon you. You now have to decide between staying late to try and catch up, or getting up even earlier tomorrow. If you stay, you'll be late for dinner or to pick up the kids from practice, and you certainly won't have time to unwind. If you leave the office now to get the gym or home to the family, you're stressed about the work left unfinished.

How did I accomplish so little? you wonder at the end of most days. *I was busy all day long...*

Being *busy* is different from being *productive.* You had great intentions and felt focused, but you let others control your time by reacting to distractions.

Tomorrow comes, and the same thing happens. It happens day after day for weeks, months, or even years. You're stuck in what seems like a never-ending cycle. Falling behind on legal work is one thing. Allowing year after year to pass with your law firm looking exactly the same is another. You're working hard, but always end up in the same spot. This is the proverbial hamster wheel that so many lawyers are on - and being honest with yourself is the only way off.

An Age-Old Problem

When you start a law firm, you don't know what you don't know. Nobody prepared you for this. How do you send out invoices? How do you grow your client base? What's a profit and loss statement? Do you need a CRM? The list goes on and on. You went to law school, not business school, and law school doesn't teach us how to run a law firm. In law school we receive world class training in how to think like a lawyer, but we were never trained on how to build a law firm business. Plus, there just aren't many established attorneys who know what they're doing *and* have the time to mentor the rest of us. It's a frustrating learning curve, and as a result, most of us fly by the seat of our pants and hope to figure it out as we go along. If we're being honest with ourselves and each other, it can have calamitous consequences.

Much of what we've learned as law firm owners is through osmosis - what we experience as young lawyers and perceive through observing others - and unfortunately, most of it is wrong. Law firms have been around for hundreds of years, and much of what you've learned about working in law is based on an outdated-by-decades model. Sure, there are timeless elements of any business, but you're trying to run a contemporary operation using practices that were built for what the world was like half a century ago, and much of the outdated model revolves around hiring and staffing. No wonder you feel stuck.

The experiences you had working for law firms early in your career didn't teach you how to get clients, how to invoice, how to do taxes, how to do your bookkeeping, or how to run the day-to-day operations. If you worked at a large firm, you learned how to bill and likely not much else. If you worked at a small firm, you probably picked up unfortunate habits from an owner who operated the same way you're operating now. At the law firm I worked for before starting my own, for example, I watched the owner organize his life by deadlines. Each day filing deadlines were discussed in the morning, and the rest of the day was like a race to beat the clock, with one emergency after another. When 4:30 p.m. hit, the paralegals had an e-filing fire drill, with all the chaos of a Wall Street trading floor and none of the upside. Maybe your's isn't quite as turbulent, but you get the drill.

You went to law school, not business school.

One of the biggest self-sabotaging habits you likely picked up, or adopted out of necessity, was taking cases outside of your dedicated practice area. You want to be a bankruptcy attorney, but you take on divorce cases because you need the revenue.

Can you imagine if this happened in any other industry?

A pediatrician wouldn't try to treat skin cancer, and a patient would never dream of asking a dermatologist to try her best at heart surgery. You're doing your clients and your reputation a disservice when you take on cases outside of your niche. That's like owning a pizza place and serving a customer who asks for a hamburger. It sounds too obvious to even point out, but just for kicks, imagine walking into a Pizza Hut and asking for a hot dog. It just feels wrong. But us lawyers, early on, we feel like clients are scarce, so we take what we can.

I get it, because I've been there. You don't know where your next case (and your next paycheck) are coming from. You were willing to take a pay cut to work for yourself, but you can't get over the initial hump to get a steady stream of appropriate clients. You talk yourself into taking cases that aren't right for you because you think it's better than nothing. You end up working way too much because you're trying to learn new areas of law on the fly, which you can't charge for. You don't have time to create systems because you're so busy just trying to get through the day. And, even if you had the time - what are systems?!

Even if you've gotten to the point where you mostly handle the right type of cases, you're working a ridiculous number of hours, but not doing nearly enough actual legal work (again, *busy* vs. *productive*). You're not alone. According to numerous studies, even with better legal software, the average solo lawyer bills less than two hours per day, and collects closer to 1.2 hours of billable work per day. That's only 15-percent of an eight-hour day. Unless you regularly stop and take stock of how you spend your time - which I know you don't, because you don't have the time! - you don't realize that you're spending the rest of your time being the firm's administrative staff.

The average solo lawyer bills less than two hours per day.

Over the years, this pattern of working long days and weekends while creating such little revenue has taken a toll on you and your family. Your spouse was excited for you when you decided to open your own law practice, and they were supportive with you every step of the way. But after a few years, the doubt starts to creep in. You had big dreams when you started out, but they're not coming true. Your practice is struggling, and you keep hoping that things will get better soon despite taking no real action or making any significant changes to the way you spend your time. But your spouse is wondering if this is what life will be like forever. Your spouse is loving and supportive, but it can be stressful to not know if your financial situation will ever improve.

Work is taking over your life, and it's affecting your relationships with your spouse and your kids. You're at work all the time, and when you're home, you're not present. You have to interrupt dinner to answer the phone because you think you can't afford to not answer a client. "My clients have my cell phone!" you've proudly announced to your networking groups and peers, "so they can reach me anytime." You have to answer emails during family movie night because you're so behind. You have to work weekends and miss your kid's sports contests. You may not mind hard work, after all, you did get through law school, but you certainly don't want to miss out on family memories because you can't keep up with your workload. In a perfect world, you would be there for your family every time. Your kids don't understand that. They just see that you're not there. Maybe they take it personally, especially if they're young. And if your spouse works, too, it's even harder on the kids. Maybe the burden is falling on your spouse, and they're not thrilled. Or maybe the impossibility of juggling your already packed work schedule with picking up the kids is driving you crazy. Your law practice is bringing tension into your home life, and this is only adding more stress onto your shoulders. I've been there. I understand.

If you're single, your law firm may be holding back your personal life, too. You're so busy trying to keep the practice afloat that you don't have time to date, spend time with friends, participate in your favorite hobbies, stay in great shape, or even just relax alone without worrying about missed emails and deadlines. Yes, you're passionate about building the law practice of your dreams, but you never envisioned your law firm would consume 90% of your life. What's worse is that your law firm isn't even at a level you consider successful yet. You're burning up your time and energy for something that's stuck.

Stress: The Silent Problem

Stress is the silent problem in law, and it manifests in many ways. No lawyer wants to admit to their clients that they're overly stressed. It would be a terrible business strategy. Clients want a lawyer who seems reliable and put-together, so you're under pressure to make it seem like everything's great, even when it's not. Admitting you're not in control goes against everything you've ever been taught about yourself and about lawyers. Maybe you can commiserate with other lawyers, but unlike many unhappy lawyers, you don't take pride in this misery.

Because you're working 24/7… you don't have time for real talks with friends, a visit to a therapist, or even alone time. If you did, you'd probably realize that everything will be okay if you take action. The real problem then, is that because you react to your day instead of controlling it, you never create the time to step back and work on your business instead of in your business.

You might not even realize how stressed you are until years down the line. You might think it's normal to feel this way all the time, but in hindsight, you'll understand how bad it really got. Your stress can disguise itself as motivation. Us lawyers are afraid of failure, and this fear drives us to get up and grind every day. If you're honest with yourself, you realize that your business has been stagnant for three, five, even ten years. Being busy gives you – or more importantly, others – the illusion that you're making progress. But the longer this cycle goes on, the more your motivation will wane. You'll lose your take-on-the-world attitude. You'll stop being excited to go to work. The lack of motivation will affect your performance, which will only make it harder to get clients.

Your stress can disguise itself as motivation.

On top of it all, running a law firm by yourself is lonely. You don't have trusted coworkers who are experiencing the stress alongside you. You don't have anyone you can talk out your business problems with. Meanwhile, you're seeing other lawyers posting their successes on social media. These lawyers might be just like you, hiding the stress under a smiling façade, but you don't know that. You feel miserable because you wonder why you can't be like them. It can be hard to get out of bed some mornings. You're so frustrated that you wonder if you need to give up and shut it down.

Or, perhaps even worse, you decide "it is what it is," and that having a small firm without many resources is what makes the most sense for you. You rationalize your reality, and decide that networking until you're 75 with one assistant or one paralegal, and maybe even a law partner who doesn't want the same things you want, is your destiny and the way life is supposed to be.

It doesn't have to be this way. Escaping may not be easy, but it really is simple; as simple as making a conscious decision to change.

There Is a Better Way

A lot of people think that all they need to build a law firm is a law degree and a laptop. They have this image of the independent lawyer working from afar, not having to answer to anyone. Yes, you can run your firm from a far off location if that's your dream, but a law firm isn't a one-person show. You need a team to help you. When you choose to run all the operations of your law firm by yourself, it is difficult to carve out even two hours a day to do legal work. Without a team in place to relieve you from wearing all the hats in the business you don't even realize you're wearing, you'll never get off the hamster wheel. Trust me, being a lawyer on the beach is a lot more fun when your law firm is helping clients, producing work and making money without you.

If you tried to open a restaurant and run it by yourself, people would say you were insane. No one person could be the host, chef, waiter, and dishwasher at the same time. The customers would have a horrible experience. And those are just the day-to-day operations. You'd never have time to consider marketing and business growth strategies. The same rings true for a law firm – it's simply not a one-person job. Yet, so many of us treat it that way. I sure did, for almost three full years. I was tired, stressed, and miserable. Only I didn't fully realize at the time just how bad it was, and I thought I could fix it by working harder and "saving" money by doing *everything* myself. I hope in that regard you're not like me.

If you're not like me, you know you need help. However, you likely don't know what to do first, and you may not believe you're at the point where you can hire someone. So many lawyers get stuck because they're afraid they don't have the money to pay an employee. They know they're drowning in endless hours of work, but the process of recruiting and hiring and training sounds daunting. What position should you hire first? Where can you find quality workers that you can afford? Would you need to rent more office space? And you're so busy...where will you find the time to go through the hiring process, let alone the money to afford that person?

I can assure you from first hand experience of growing my law firm from true solo to over 40 employees, the only way to get out from under this heap of redundancy you've created is to perform fewer functions in your firm. You heard that right. You *need* to do less. Every law firm (and business), at their core, has marketing, sales, HR, production, and finance needs, amongst many, many others. Unless you have people filling these seats, you're performing these duties for your firm. Please understand this concept. It's not that you don't have a marketing, sales or finance director. You're the marketing director, and you're failing miserably at your job. If someone offered you a job as the marketing, sales, HR and finance director all at once, outside of being paid an outlandish sum, would you take the job? No, you wouldn't.

You're the marketing director for your firm, and you're failing miserably at your job.

As I will fully explain in this book along with providing a road map out, if you don't start hiring help and firing yourself from these roles, you're dooming yourself to the feast or famine cycle forever. The cycle where you hustle and network, get a few clients, spend your time working on those matters, and then when you're done, because you've been working and not networking, you have no more clients, so you run out and hustle and do it all again.

I'm here to show you a way out of this cycle—and it's easier than you think. Whether you're a true solo or have a partner but no staff, have a "paralegal" who also wears too many hats, or a few employees but your last new hire was more than a year ago, this book is for you. If you want to bring in more revenue and actually keep some of it, keep reading. If you're overwhelmed, overworked, over stressed and underpaid, these pages will be a pot of gold. We're giving you the road map to build your virtual law firm team step-by-step over the next 24 months. This team is going to make you super productive, and comes without needing more office space and about one-third of the cost of hiring locally. Your staff will be friendly and will appreciate you for the job. Your firm will start to run like a machine, allowing you to finally get off the hamster wheel and discover the *Liberated Lawyer Lifestyle.*

CHAPTER 2

The Law Firm Grind (And Your Escape Plan)

I have a law degree, you may be thinking, *my life and income should be more stable than this.*

The glory days when a law degree *guaranteed* an upper-middle-class life are over in the United States. The old adage of "just do a good job and clients will find you" doesn't work anymore. There's too much competition. It's the reality of supply and demand. Anybody can achieve success if you put in the work, but the days of opening your doors in a small town and doing everyone's legal work for 40 years without any real competitive threats are gone with the wind.

The Way Out

Don't give in to despair. I've seen many law firm owners almost give up when they were three feet from gold. You might be beating yourself up thinking that you're just not cut out for owning a law firm, but that's not true; you're thinking about your business in the wrong way - or not thinking about your firm as a business at all. The great news is that you're capable of running a terrific and profitable law firm with a small shift in the way you're thinking about and running the business.

Realizing this concept is crucially important, because it can allow you to decide to change. Thousands of lawyers across the world own successful, profitable law firms that provide the owner(s) a great lifestyle. You can't argue with that fact. You're a smart, hard working lawyer—once you learn how to run the firm, your practice will flourish, and your stress will start to dissipate. I know because I've been there, and I've done it.

Time is infinitely more valuable than money, especially at this juncture in your business.

The good news for you is that I'm going to give you a clear and straightforward way out. The path is to buy back your time. Time is infinitely more valuable than money, especially at this juncture in your business. You might be afraid that you can't afford to hire, but you'll never make money until you do.

How do you buy back your time? You hire staff. Plain and simple. You fire yourself from wearing specific hats in your firm as soon as humanly possible. We're giving you the formula in this book.

Afraid of hiring or think you can't afford it? Worry not. Here's the best part. You can hire staff for a third of the price that you're accustomed to who are every bit as qualified and competent as you're used to, and in many cases, even more competent. Who am I referring to?

The answer is offshore employees. You'd be hard pressed to find an industry not utilizing offshore/international team members. These employees are fully virtual – no office space (i.e. overhead) required. Hiring extremely competent and friendly staff members at a cost that reduces stress instead of compounding it is, quite frankly, life changing. I'm going to show you who to hire, what order to hire them in, and what to look for when hiring – in a way that you can afford. In a way that instead of leading to more stress, you'll start to taste some freedom.

When you embark on the hiring process and try to do it yourself, it's hard. Each time you hire, it takes anywhere from 8 to 14 months of placing ads, recruiting, interviewing, hiring, training, regretting, firing, and then doing it all over again, before you finally find someone halfway decent. Have you ever tried to hire someone and it goes terribly wrong? Of course! We all have. Every one of us has those horror stories. Or, worse yet, have you ever held onto the wrong person for too long because the thought of going through all of that again is terrifying? Yup, and you're not alone. As Tim Ferriss (of *The 4-Hour Work Week* fame) says, it takes on average seven tries to find a good assistant when you hire on your own. So what we all tend to do is not hire someone because it takes too much time, instead hoping someone great falls out of the sky onto our lap. *Maybe your colleague with whom you share space will have a niece or nephew looking for a job*, you think to yourself, on month 16 of not having that help you need. Even if you do realize that every business has needs and you can't do it all alone, taking the correct action is the difference between freedom and misery. For reasons unknown, most people never consider there's a better way to hire than to do it yourself, especially when you first get started hiring. I've been through it before, and I can help you avoid wasting gobs of time and money.

I've built a process that reliably produces the top 1% of the English-speaking international workforce. Highly educated, highly motivated individuals wanting to make a great living right where they live by working as your virtual employee. That realization is the only thing holding you back from the life you want. When you start to get these virtual team members on your staff, you'll *finally* have time to focus on tasks that move the business forward, and that's when everything will start to get better.

I often say that the best part of this line of business is the lives that we've been able to change for people in other countries. You truly change lives when you hire offshore. Instead of having to leave their home countries and everything they've ever known to travel to America and seek a better life, virtual team members (also known as Staffers) get to stay where they are and build a life. We've witnessed so many of our people get married, buy a house and start a family, all while being extremely grateful for their employment. As a company, we guarantee our Staffers that even if their first employer doesn't work out, we'll do everything in our power to re-match them. We're getting better every day, as is the quality of the highly educated people we recruit. So, if just one person gets a job as a result of me writing this book and convincing someone to hire offshore, it will have been worth every bit of effort.

Some people may disagree with what I've said so far and argue that before you start hiring you need to have a plan of exactly where you're going. What I know is that by hiring no one, your plan doesn't matter because you're going to get pretty much where you are today. Wherever you're going, you can't get there alone, and if you have a plan, that plan will include hiring help or it's worthless. Very few actions in your firm cannot be undone, and you'll learn far more from the journey than you will staying at home spending months trying to put it all on paper. There are five stages of entrepreneurship, and the only way to get out of the first stage - which should be everyone's goal - is hiring. Let's discuss.

The Five Stages of Entrepreneurship

Broadly speaking, there are five stages of entrepreneurship for the business owner: *Hustler, Experimenter, Visionary, Systemizer*, and *Influencer*. First of all, make no mistake, if you started a law firm, even if you never thought about it this way or don't see yourself this way, you're an entrepreneur (or a *lawpreneur*, if you prefer). Second of all, your goal should be to mature from one stage to the next as quickly yet prudently as possible. Why? Because the hustle stage is exhausting, and each stage is exponentially more fun than the previous stage. Let me explain.

The *Hustler* is a true solo and does everything herself. Nothing happens without the *Hustler*, causing exhaustion, chaos, or severe stagnation. Think of one juggler managing seven balls (consultations, depositions, drafting and e-filing all in one day, anyone?). When she stops juggling, which she must at some point, the balls drop, and the show crashes to a screeching halt. The way out of this stage is to stop hustling. How can you stop hustling, however, when your business has needs? Ah yes, employees. Someone else to juggle some of the balls for you.

Make a few good hires, train them and then let them do work, and you graduate to *Experimenter*. The *Experimenter* has created limited time to work on the business, but every employee reports to him. There is more breathing room, but the business is fickle. The *Visionary* has made more key hires and has the ability to delegate and focus both on the business and also on the higher value tasks than before. The *Visionary* can potentially start to delegate sales, which is the true test of whether a business can survive without the owner. While working on the business, the *Visionary* now has time to truly create the business of his or her dreams and set the vision and destination for what's to come. The *Systemizer* is focused on creating a leadership team and processes to run the firm. With a leadership team and systems in place, the *Influencer* emerges. The *Influencer* can spread the message, write books and speak on stages, navigate growth opportunities and mitigate risks. As stated above, this is truly a wonderful place to get to.

Growing through the five stages of entrepreneurship seems so easy when it's on paper. However, there is no easy button in life. And we're not concerned with growing through all five stages in this book. Let's walk before we run. This book is designed to get you ready for that Visionary stage where you can start to taste the *Freedom Lawyer Lifestyle*, with the time freedom to act as a *Visionary* as you move to *Systemizer*. This is where your business plan starts to matter. When you're real small, it's easy to course correct. When you start to grow and work on the business, decisions become more critical. But growing a business to the point where you have freedom doesn't have to be as complicated as others make it seem.

There is no easy button in life.

Make no mistake - I'm a huge believer in finding and paying for the right (i.e., high quality and experienced) coaching. I'm an even bigger fan of a great mastermind. Finding a great coach and a great mastermind are two of the main factors in my own success story. That said, whether you have a marketing coach selling you marketing services because marketing and leads are sexy, an intake coach helping you fix the biggest leaky bucket most firms don't realize they have, or a legal coach helping you analyze how many leads you need to meet your professional goals, they all lead back to one road: You must find, hire, train and maintain good people to get out of the *Hustler* and *Experimenter* stages and into the *Visionary* stage of your business. Bottom line.

Now, is that all you must do? No. But you don't need to know exactly where you're going before you get started, either. You don't need to know the *exact* number of leads you need this year, because whether it's three or three hundred, you need at least one person doing your intake, one person answering your phones, one person helping drive leads, one person helping manage your books and invoicing, and one person to protect your time. You know you need more leads and to convert those leads, and without assistance, you're simply hustling from one lead to the next. By hiring people to help in these roles, you're going to get and convert more leads into paying clients. Again, it doesn't matter if it's three or three hundred, you just need more to get out of the *Hustler* (true solo) stage.

I've yet to meet a *true* solo attorney who (1) isn't miserably stressed or (2) has a real business that can run without him or her that also provides the financial means necessary for that lawyer to live a great life. If you can introduce me to one, I'll buy you lunch. What hiring the right people means, is hiring someone who fits in your firm's culture (let's keep it simple for now - do you like that person and do they give you energy or do they drain you), who is competent and who is coachable. That's it, in a nutshell. Then, once you find that person, you must learn how to be a boss. You must learn how to manage that person, give them feedback, give them a structure with objective criteria so they actually know if they're doing a good job. Yes, you must learn how to become a leader who is comfortable in your own skin. You must hold your team accountable, but also respect them and the relationship you each have with your firm.

Suffice to say that there are no unicorns - you won't simply make these next hires and from day one they step into your firm and do everything you've ever dreamed of. If life were that easy, it wouldn't be any fun. When you buy your time back though, you spend it learning a little bit more about what your business needs and on driving more revenue, so you can make another hire, free up some more of your time, learn how to train and manage that person, then rinse and repeat. Once you're entering the *Visionary* stage, maybe you join a mastermind or a guild. Maybe you travel to conferences. Maybe you get a CEO. Whatever it is - hiring isn't an easy button, but without a few good people and some resources and bandwidth, you'll be stuck hustling and you won't have time to execute on coaching anyway.

You must find, hire, train and maintain good people to get out of the Hustler and Experimenter stages and into the Visionary stage of your business. Bottom line.

I would be remiss if I didn't also talk about the really fun part as well - that *Influencer* stage. One day you'll have grown your team enough that you no longer need to do the training yourself. Then you get to offload the legal work. Then the management of the team. Then you get to focus on what you truly want to do with your time. For some, that's to be a great trial lawyer. For others, that's to work while traveling the world, never wearing a suit again. And still for others, that's to keep growing because life is too short to play small. To each his or her own. That's the process as I've seen it - first, hire some amazing people so you're not alone, then invest in learning how to really grow your firm, then reach the point where you get to change the world.

Getting to Why

What do I know, and why listen to me, you rightfully ask? I started a law firm in late 2011 that's now a 12-attorney law firm with over 40 total team members, 16 of whom are offshore in Latin America. That firm has a leadership team and runs with highly compensated, highly talented individuals at the helm, mostly without me. Is it perfect? Of course not, but our growth has been admirable, and we're also on the cusp of some even bigger things.

Many other firms with fabulous owners whom I know and respect have become much bigger much faster than mine. Many others haven't. It matters not; what matters is that you believe it's possible. You're not in a race with others, you're in a race with yourself.

I'm also CEO and Co-Founder of Get Staffed Up (GSU), the legal field's largest and fastest growing virtual staffing company. At the time of publication, we have over 160 employees, 95% of which are offshore. Between the two companies, we've reached the Inc. 5000 list four times, and GSU hit the top 100. Why do I mention these successes? I do believe credibility matters, and who you listen to matters. We're lawyers, after all. We're skeptical. So, I am giving you some of my business resume and achievements to make three final points before we dive in:

First, if I can do it, so can you. I promise. There's nothing special or different about me. I wasn't born into a wealthy family, went to a college most people have never heard of, and didn't get an MBA. I was lost my first few years, stressed out of my mind, and looking back - was flat-out miserable. I wish I had realized sooner that everything would be okay. I just needed to meet the right people, read the right books, and take action. I hope this book is one of those game changers for you.

Second, growth shows proof of concept and market acceptance. GSU wouldn't be scaling if we weren't finding amazing people for terrific law firm owners all across the United States, and those firms wouldn't be growing through their entrepreneurial stages like they are if the staffers we find weren't exceptional team members. You can't fake your way into the size of company we've become. We are helping lawyers all across North America staff up with amazing talent from the rest of the Americas. Those lawyers whom we're helping grow often get asked how they're doing it, and the smart ones who listen and believe what they see then become our clients. It's a lot of fun.

Third and finally, you can sum up my philosophy of success quite succinctly: it's the people. Other than your family, you'll spend most of your precious time on this earth, at least at this stage of your life, with your work team. Don't tolerate anything but amazing people who are willing to learn. Adopt the mindset that while your team may work for you, you keep earning them every day. Hire great people, train them, and then let them do their thing. Delegation isn't a dirty word - why hire someone just to micromanage them? Let them make your business and your life better, and you'll both be better off.

At this point I've done my best to paint the reality of what life probably looks like for you to some varying degree, and I hope you're honest with the one person with whom it really matters you be honest with - yourself. So many lawyers I know have every excuse in the book for why their law firm hasn't changed or grown in years. I hope you choose not to be one of them. I've also painted the picture of how great life can look on the other side - when you take extreme ownership of yourself and your circumstances, realize there will be lots of learning and micro failures along the stages of entrepreneurship, and you focus on becoming the person - and law firm owner - you really want to be.

What matters to you and what's your *why*? Why do you do what you do? You may have an inkling, a strong purpose, or you haven't thought about it too much. In any event, before you get out of *Hustle* and *Experiment*, it's not as important. Dreaming isn't as fun while you can't pay the bills. Our goal here is to get you to the point where, 24 months from now as a budding *Visionary*, you can get to *why*. Follow our plan, and you'll most assuredly get there.

The Path to Freedom

There are very predictable needs and patterns for a growing law firm. In the rest of this book, we're going to get granular. We're going to outline the hires, the economics behind the hires, the tasks and duties the hires will do for you, the characteristics of the hires you need to make, and where those hires - if properly managed (properly is a loaded term, to be sure, but this is where you take extreme responsibility for being a good employer) - will take your firm financially, give or take a few dollars. We also have landing pages for each chapter with additional resources to guide you through these hires. If you have a coach, are part of a program, or are in a mastermind, please share. They should be thrilled with this book and these resources. The "people business" is the toughest business, especially in this day and age. We're here to help you take action.

Show me your calendar, and I'll show you your future. Change in life always comes back to how we spend our time. Most of us don't plan our days though, we let our days control us. How do we know your life won't magically change without making the decision to change and then taking action? Take everything you did last week, and put it on your calendar for next week. (I'm serious, this is a powerful exercise). Would you choose to live the rest of your life this way? Answering emails all day, letting interruptions control your plans, and distractions interfere with progress? I hope not. And if it sounds like I'm condemning you here - I do this exercise quarterly, deciding what new activities aren't serving me and what to delegate, eliminate or automate next. I'm not condemning in the least bit, I'm hoping that this illustration helps spur you to realize that without making a change, nothing changes.

The main difference between you and the lawyers who you admire, even if you secretly begrudge them because you know you're a better lawyer, is just how they spend their time. Fix how you spend your time, and everything else will start to take care of itself. On the other side of taking accountability that you and you alone are responsible for your business, making a decision that you're worth it, committing to change, and then taking calculated action to grow, is the Liberated Lawyer Lifestyle of a *Visionary* law firm owner. The freedom to do you. How and what and when and why. Sound liberating? It is. And you can get there in 24 months. Let's dive in.

PART II

24 Months to Freedom

CHAPTER 3

If You Don't Have an Assistant, You Are the Assistant

I was at an event one time where I heard the speaker say something incredibly profound: "If you don't have an assistant, you are the assistant."

For some reason, most of us lawyers never consider hiring someone when we open our law firm. Maybe that's true for a lot of service businesses. Even so, it's a mistake. When your business has a total of one employees (i.e., you) instead of working on your cases or working on developing cases, you find yourself answering the phone, e-filing, running errands, trying to return phone calls, terrified of your email inbox and what you might miss, all while trying to keep your clients updated, opposing counsel under control, the court informed, and the lights on.

In other words, you're not only wearing every hat, you're spending most of your day with the secretary hat on, earning your firm about $10 an hour. If you want to be a handyman who works by the hour and goes home after a hard day's work - and I'm not criticizing anyone, my handyman is extremely valuable to me - then working all by yourself makes sense. But I implore you to consider your law firm more like a real business that just happens to be owned by you and employs you as a lawyer (and in lots of other roles, for now).

We've established that you didn't go to law school to be miserable. Not you. You already invested in yourself by paying for college and a law degree. You're ready to make a good living and live a decent life, which you can do because you have that degree. You passed the bar. You're qualified to do legal work and charge at least $300 an hour. Why on earth would you waste your day doing work that only pays $10 an hour?

You have eight hours in a workday, and as an entrepreneur, while not ideal long term, you probably work closer to 11 to 12 hours a day. Think about how much money you're losing by not filling more of those hours with legal work. If you can bill $300 an hour doing billable work, every 10 minutes you spend on admin work loses you $50. Yes, that's $50 you're losing, every 10 minutes, and you're likely billing more than $300 per hour to begin with.

Before you tell yourself (1) I don't have eight hours of legal work in a day or (2) I'm a contingency fee or flat fee lawyer, consider that you likely have much more legal work than you think, you've just been too busy answering phones and worrying about your next client to focus on working the cases you do have. (And if you're a PI attorney, your hour is worth the same if not more, even if you don't bill by the hour).

In either scenario, wouldn't it be much better to have an actual secretary do the secretarial work (because your business needs these tasks done, you can't simply ignore them) while you focus on the matters you do have? Even if you thought twice as hard about how to win a litigation matter, or settle a bankruptcy matter, or pop an insurance policy, or create a better trust and then a program for updating your clients' wills every year, wouldn't that be better time spent than any of the secretarial duties we've listed already?

Of course it would.

Now that we've decided you're costing yourself and your firm $50 for every ten minutes you act as your own assistant, which in my experience is probably around four to five hours a day and therefore $1,200 - $1,500 a day when you consider all of the administrative tasks you perform for your firm, let's talk about what a great assistant will make you (notice I didn't say cost you, because good employees don't cost you money, they make you money). You can hire a virtual assistant for less than $100 a day to take 90% of these tasks off your hands.

Doubling Your Revenue - It's (Much) Easier Than You Think

Lots of experts with all the answers will pretend like growing your business is easy. Remember, I said it's simple, not easy. All you have to do is work on your business, they'll say, without a hint of self-awareness that as a consultant they've never grown a business themselves. Contrary to popular belief, it is okay to work in your business as a lawyer...as long as you're doing legal work. Your goal should be to fire and replace yourself from each and every role you have as soon as possible, with the last role either being the CEO or being the lawyer, depending on your preference.

But doubling your revenue early on is actually pretty straightforward. The typical solo attorney bills an average of 1 to 1.2 hours per day. I used to think this was way off, but the numbers bear it out. With our conservative example of $300/hour, that's about $360 per day, $1,820 a week and with about 22 working days in each month, just under $8,000 a month and about $100,000 a year. When I was completely on my own, I averaged about $9,000 a month, give or take. Most solo attorneys I've spoken to are/were about the same. Perhaps it's a bit more today, or you're in a larger city with higher rates, but considering cost of living, the net effect is relative.

Here comes the mind-blowingly simple fact that still pains me because I spent over two and a half years stuck at this level without realizing it: In order to double your revenue, you only need to double your billable hours.

That's it.

How difficult would it be to bill 2 to 2.4 hours in a day? Do an hour in the morning and an hour in the afternoon. It's simple math, and yet the solution is so elusive for most of us. First, we tell ourselves that although 1.2 times 2 equals 2.4, life doesn't really work that way. (Hint, mathematically speaking it does, and as you grow, understanding your numbers and the mechanics of your firm becomes more and more important). We also tell ourselves, okay, but I don't need to hire someone to get more work done, I'll just buckle down and focus more and do it. But we don't, because a business needs what a business needs and us humans can't sustainably change our spots. Probably like you, I thought that one day I would just get more work done, and I avoided hiring someone for far too long.

In order to double your revenue, you only need to double your billable hours.

Here's my story. When I finally decided to hire someone for the first time, I was terrified that I wouldn't be able to pay them. I hired a law student to assist me for 30 hours a week, thinking that if I hired a law student and it didn't work out, it would be easy to let her go. I had no idea how I was going to pay her, not realizing the simple math of what was about to happen (when we're stressed about money, emotion controls our decision making, not logic). As mentioned, I was doing about $9,000 a month in revenue at this time.

The very first month I had the assistant, I brought in $20,000. I couldn't believe it. I more than doubled my revenue, and I didn't even have to get more clients. So I traded about $1,500 for $11,000. What a deal. I was finally able to do more work each month for the clients I already had—the work I should've been doing all along but didn't have time to get to and bill. Remember when I said you have more legal work than you think you do? Think about it: if you have five clients and only have time for legal work one hour a day, you only have one hour a week to devote to each client. Kind of crazy when you break it down that way.

Is my story an outlier? Not hardly. We see it all the time.

"We're able to bill more hours than we ever could before."

At our small family law firm, we had a part-time in-person staffer who handled phone calls and calendaring when they were in, but often one of the two attorneys would have to answer phone calls, calendar appointments, and coordinate meetings–all non-billable activities. **We were constantly interrupted by calls and distracted by calendar issues. It made our work days fragmented,** and it made it hard to get traction on important–and billable–client matters.

We did not want to hire a generic answering service, as that can be off-putting to clients. We needed someone who would serve as our first line of contact for those things but be a member of the team and make clients feel comfortable. After hearing positive things about GSU staffers from colleagues, **we interviewed & hired a virtual assistant. From the moment we saw her video, we had a sense that she would be a fit for the firm,** and we hoped her skill set matched her fantastic personality (it did!). Almost instantly, we felt our efficiency improve. **Our assistant immediately settled in, became familiar with our**

client management software and firm practices, and began handling numerous daily tasks like scheduling and emails.

Once we implemented a VOIP phone system, she could answer and screen calls, perform client intake, schedule and confirm appointments, take messages when we didn't want to be interrupted, and help keep us focused. As her familiarity with the practice has grown, she has taken on more responsibilities, which allows us to focus on billable work. She always looks ahead and ensures that we are prepared for deadlines, meetings, and court appearances. Sometimes she will have something already handled for us - calendaring the details of a Zoom meeting and sending the document to a mediator, for example - before we even ask! She is kind, patient, and professional with our clients, which is reassuring for us when we cannot speak to the clients ourselves. **Our practice is more organized, we're more productive, and we're able to bill more hours than we ever could before.**

- Katherine Richardson, Esq., Richardson & Richardson, LLC

Like Katherine, a smart use of your first assistant is a little bit of everything. If you make this hire and stop there, well, I can proudly say we accomplished something. But hopefully you won't because there's more. A lot, lot more.

The Barriers to Hiring An Executive Assistant

Maybe you don't think you have enough work to fill 40 hours of a virtual assistant's time. That's not true. I've never met any law firm owner who couldn't fill 40 hours of an employee's time. You're underestimating how much of your own time needs to be freed up, and you likely have never sat down and put pen to paper to write out all of the things you're doing that could and should be handled by someone else.

Think about this. When you need to schedule a call with somebody, you email them, they email you back, you email them again, they email you back, and you email them again. It takes about 30 minutes of back-and-forth over email to schedule a 15-minute call. Then, you have to take an extra five minutes to put the call on your calendar, send them the calendar invite, and make sure it was done the right way. Now multiply that by 10-20 times per week. This is just one short example of the small ways that time leaks add up.

Imagine if you could sit and do legal work while your new virtual assistant handles all of that scheduling (even Calendly needs a human paying attention, let's be honest - delegating that just to get the worry of missing calls and scheduling is worth it for the headspace it'll save you). When the call actually does happen, the phone is answered in a friendly fashion, and patched over to you, who is all ready for the call because your Executive Assistant prepped you for the call earlier that day or five minutes before it happened. You've now saved 30 cumulative minutes of time by having someone else schedule one call for you. Thirty minutes on one call? Sounds absurd, but maybe now it makes sense that solo attorneys only bill 1.2 hours per day.

Here are 12 easy ways (out of 100) that you can free your time and fill your new Executive Assistant's workload:

1. Managing your email
2. Managing your calendar
3. Scheduling meetings, lunches, calls, etc.
4. Sending important clients personalized emails
5. Placing outbound calls to check in with clients

6. E-filing
7. Tracking your time
8. Taking notes during consultations
9. Light marketing/social media tasks
10. Networking coordination
11. Preparing bills and invoicing clients
12. Booking reservations

The above is plenty to get started with, and should easily fill 40 hours of someone's time, even if you're just starting out. But let's say, worst case scenario, your Executive Assistant has a few extra hours a week to help with special projects, maybe? Because we've already agreed that every 10 minutes you spend doing assistant work yourself costs you $50.00, you should hire a full-time executive assistant even if you're afraid you won't be able to fill *all* their time.

Full-Time or Hourly?

A quick rant on hourly hiring.

When you hire an assistant on an hourly basis for 10 or 20 hours a week, by nature that worker isn't dedicated to you because they need to fill their time and earning capacity working for someone else to fill the rest of their time. You never know when you're going to need your assistant, and in many instances they'll be working for someone else when you need them.

Because most lawyers, like me, underestimate the time it takes to complete tasks, with an hourly person you never feel like you're getting what you pay for. Every day you're waiting until it's your turn with them to get answers to your questions and updates on assignments.

The last thing you want is to lose momentum because you're waiting until your $10/hour assistant is on the clock to contact them. It's just not worth it. Your time is too valuable. And, as we've discussed, every hour they don't work for you is really costing you $250.00.

So, unless you're a part-time lawyer with part-time clients who wants part-time results, don't do this to yourself. You're better than that, and you're worth it. So are your clients.

There's nothing wrong with having a good team member with a little bit of extra capacity. You don't want your virtual assistant to work 50 hours a week. You want them to have enough time to get things done when you need them done. So if you can't fill 40 hours exactly, don't worry. The time will get occupied as projects come up each day. There will always be something to help with. It's better to book someone as a full-time employee to guarantee their loyalty and commitment than to be scrambling when your part-time worker is gone and you need a million things done.

Your first assistant will likely be a jack of all trades.

Your executive assistant will by necessity be a jack of all trades. Their purpose is to buy you back your time. When you get further down the line, you'll want to hire different people with more specific skill sets and roles, but for now you just need someone to take things off your plate so you can do more legal work. Focus on doubling your output. Don't overthink it.

Your first executive assistant should be someone that you like to work with, as you're going to spend a lot of virtual time with them. You should hit it off in the interview. You're going to spend a lot of time working with this person, so you want to make sure you'll be happy to see them on Zoom each day. If you're not excited to work with this person, your lawyer-assistant partnership will fail. If they have a bad attitude, you'll dread delegating tasks to them because you'd rather just not deal with it, and it'll get in the way of your progress. You can reject mediocrity while having realistic expectations at the same time. You'll find that balance as you learn and grow.

You want your executive assistant to have a wide array of skills but be especially adept at email and managing calendars. This person should be smart, organized, and trustworthy. When you're hiring, the best rule is to go with your gut. And if you hire someone and they don't turn out to be good at the job, you have to move on sooner rather than later. Don't blame yourself or stress too much if you hire someone who doesn't work out— just move on quickly. It's not a failure, it's a learning experience, and you're on to the next one without a loss of enthusiasm - because you realize that this one hire will cost you just under $500 a week and make you about $10,000 per month.

Chapter Recap

After hiring your executive assistant, you'll wonder how you ever lived without one. You'll wish it was always this easy to double your revenues, you're excited about hiring, and have decided that growth may not be such a scary idea after all. By offloading the administrative tasks that interfered with your focus, you created the time to be a real lawyer with real results.

24 Months to Freedom Roadmap

First Hire: Executive Assistant

Investment: $1,995/month

Firm Revenues Before Hire: $8,500/month

Firm Revenues After Hire: $17,000/month

Net Gain: $6,505/month (Increased revenue minus cost of hire)

Total Gain: $6,505/month

Hiring and Training Timetable: Months One through Three

For more information on how to hire an executive assistant, a sample weekly scorecard and more, please visit qrco.de/executive-assistant or scan this QR code now:

At the end of each chapter in Part II, we're providing a sample 24-month journey of a typical law firm following our roadmap. Realizing that the numbers can't be exact (and hopefully, because you're wearing your law firm *owner* hat not *lawyer* hat, you realize they don't need to be), you can see how each hire is going to change your firm and the timeline associated therewith. The investment means the hard cost of the new, incredible, full-time, offshore team member you hired, the net gain is the increased profit in that month (increased revenue minus cost of the hire), and the total gain is the aggregate increase in profit for your firm after each hire compounds. Again, every firm is different, so the numbers won't be exact. But they should be close.

The timeline should also be very close if you follow the plan in this book, with each hire ranging from two to four months to onboard and train, culminating at 24 months. If you do the sourcing, recruiting, interviewing and hiring yourself for each position, add another 15 months on the low end and 30 months on the high end to the timeline.

CHAPTER 4

Your Biggest First Impression

A receptionist is your business's biggest first impression...

Yes, receptionists are still vital, even in the digital age. Explaining why receptionists (and your intake system overall, which we'll get to soon) are absolutely critical for a law firm to be successful is one of my favorites past times. Yet, some lawyers just won't get it and will opt for shortcuts instead. I'm hoping to obliterate that nonsensical thinking once and for all.

Why go out and network and spend money marketing, only to miss calls and/or fail to follow up with leads? A friend of mine calls this problem (which he wrote a book about) *The Golden Toilet* - flushing all those marketing dollars right down the toilet because you don't have a thoughtful plan on what to do when the marketing and networking actually works. That plan begins with hiring a fantastic receptionist, and no, not a receptionist service.

There are three huge problems with not hiring a full-time dedicated receptionist who answers the phone the right way, the same way, and with a cheery attitude that makes people want to call you, every time.

- Missed calls.
- Not responding to potential new clients quickly enough.

- The poor impression that an answering service creates in the minds of your clients and potential clients.

Why Receptionists Are as Essential as Ever

You're an attorney, and the chances are slim that you never have to talk to clients on the phone. Even if your clients reach out to you mostly via email, you'll need to get them on the phone at some point. And many clients still want to speak with you directly, especially if they have a problem.

Your phone *will* ring, and you *will* need someone to answer it. If you don't have a receptionist, your clients will get the impression that you're a small-time law firm who must not be successful because you can't afford to hire someone to answer the phone. They'll assume that you must not be busy because you have time to get on the phone yourself.

But when a lawyer is inaccessible, it gives the client the impression of prestige. You're an important, successful lawyer whose time is valuable and requires an appointment.

Most law firms employ receptionists, so if you don't have one, it sticks out to the client, and not in a good way. But when someone else answers your phone for you, it'll put you on the same playing field as more established law firms that the client is considering.

When you think of a receptionist, you probably think of the person sitting behind a fancy desk when you walk into an office. Even though that's not the way the world looks anymore, you still need a receptionist.

The person at the desk isn't the important part, it's the phones that matter. If your law firm is fully virtual, you especially need a full-time receptionist. Humans have problems, and they call lawyers. Even if they initially fill out a form, they still want to speak to someone to understand the process and how their problem will be handled.

And if you have a front desk where clients and potential clients still come to the office, great. Someone can greet them. But to get to that point, 99% of the time, they will have called your office first, at least once, if not multiple times. People don't walk into law firms off the street, except maybe in really, really small towns. They look you up online and then pick up the phone and call. This call is the first impression your client will get of your business.

First Problem - Missing the Call

Missing a call is one of the worst things you can do for your business. Forget missing a call which could have been your next big case for now, the impression it leaves on existing clients is also terrible. Have I made a mistake and hired a poor lawyer? Is my lawyer now screening my calls? Isn't there someone else at the firm who can handle my question? Like it or not, that's what your clients think when you inevitably don't answer their phone calls.

Have you ever met the proud-yet-misguided attorney who brags that their clients have their *personal* cell phone number? First of all, giving your clients your cell number only leads to misery. With all due respect even to our biggest and best clients, no boundaries equals an awful life. Plus, your client will respect you a lot more as a professional if you have a functioning staff and well-run business so that they don't need your personal cell number, unless it's to invite you on a fun outing. Second, the lawyer who beams with pride as they make this boastful claim is likely missing most of their calls anyway!

What self-respecting attorney out there kicking butt and taking names has the time to answer their phone? None. Which is why they miss calls and frustrate their clients. Are they well-intentioned? Maybe. They could also be lying to themselves and telling themselves that they're so important that no one else can handle the call.

I see this most often with criminal defense attorneys, and many get outright defensive when I suggest that they'd land more cases with a full-time remote receptionist. Does a criminal defense attorney need the phones answered every time in order to not miss a case? Absolutely. Someone in trouble doesn't have time to wait around for a new attorney whom they've never met to answer their phone. They're scared, and need help now. Who answers the phone when a criminal defense lawyer is in court? After all, they must be in court representing all those clients, right? What does a person in trouble with the law think when the attorney they were recommended answers their own phone? *Must not be very busy with very many cases*, that's what. Try charging a premium after creating that impression.

Any lawyer who loves court shouldn't weed out mental distractions, the easiest of which is the worry of missing out on the next case because no one is covering your phones, taking messages and following up with leads. I still remember that amazing feeling of leaving court and not having my stomach in my throat wondering how many calls and emails I missed. This is the precise reason to have a full-time receptionist. Rain, shine, court, vacation, family event, mental clarity break, you name it - your phones need to be answered, and unless someone other than you is doing the answering, you'll not only miss calls, the stress of having to tend to your phone will exacerbate the problem. The first time you get out of a hearing, and receive a message from your receptionist that they set up a call, consultation, or even new case for you while you were working, will be a literal life changing event.

Second problem - Missing your next case because you took too long to respond

Back to the golden toilet. Research shows that if you miss a call, or someone merely takes a message for you but is an outside receptionist so they can't schedule a call back or answer even simple questions, and you or someone from your firm take more than five minutes to contact that potential new client, the chances that you land them drop to an absurdly low percentage, something like less than 10%. Nobody has time to wait on a law firm who can't return calls or email inquiries. If five minutes have passed, they'll already have looked up the next firm and placed the call. You may not like this rule, but it's true.

The same goes for online inquiries. The odds that someone fills out a form on your website and only your website are miniscule. You may think you're the greatest lawyer ever, but to the market, you look decent online, as do many others. Potential clients are testing the waters to see which law firms are the most responsive, even if they don't implicitly know it. Responsiveness implies professionalism, organization, and trust. That's the law firm people want.

Another telling statistic: Up to 50% of sales goes to the firm that responds first. Tired of that "other lawyer" getting all the cases? Here's why. They respond first. If you don't have a receptionist (and later an intake specialist) monitoring online inquiries and picking up the phone to respond immediately, another law firm has beaten you to the punch and you and the other five firms who eventually respond will be fighting for the scraps.

Lawyers who insist they can be great lawyers, spend adequate time to think through and then execute on a client's case in order to win, plus answer their own phones and respond to online inquiries baffle me. We all got into law school by passing a big logic exam, and yet here we are - illogically making up rules or exceptions in our minds when we try to run our firms. Again, I'm not being unfairly harsh on anyone, because I have no room to speak. I did it for almost three years.

You cannot be a good lawyer, work on your matters, answer your own phones and respond to online inquiries. You need a full-time receptionist. Show me how you spend your time, and I'll show you your future.

Third Problem - Answering "Services"

So you agree trying to answer your own phones is not only insanity but it's costing you cases, time and money. You're all in. Yet now you want to hire... an answering service? With the risk of blowback from my friends in the answering service business, there is a time and place for these companies, and that place if for backup and after hours, only. But answering services aren't all created equally. Most of them should be called answering disservices, unfortunately. Why? Answering service businesses are a challenge to scale, and that challenge becomes your problem.

When you have a full-time receptionist, your phone can be answered the same way, every time. You can hire a cheery, happy-to-hear-from-you person who makes clients feel all fuzzy inside. After all, you're in business to help people, surely you want to hear from those people, right? Your dedicated receptionist will know how to pronounce your name, will have your personal calendar available and know your whereabouts. They will know all the right questions to ask when taking a message.

They will get to know each of your clients individually, and can handle many client inquiries without even bothering you. They can assure potential clients that they've called the right place, make them feel good about reaching out, and set up a call back or handle the next steps. They can also place the client briefly on hold while your on-hold message educates the caller about all the other great things your law firm does. A good receptionist is soothing to clients and calming to the rest of the firm. You have enough challenges in your law firm, this doesn't need to be one of them.

An answering service cannot *reliably* do any of these things, despite what they promise.

You cannot be a great lawyer, work on your matters, answer your own phones and respond to online inquiries.

When using an answering service, someone new answers your phone every time, and oftentimes they don't know how to pronounce your name or the name of the law firm. They don't know where you are, so you're relying on them to follow the instructions for properly taking a message.

You're also relying on them to relay that message to you in a timely fashion. Can all this be done in five minutes? And yet still, who is calling the potential new client back anyway?

Some services promise to set up consultations and do callbacks for you. Have you ever had someone call you back and try to follow a script and the first time you ask a question that person has no clue how to answer? It's an answering service.

Client and potential client interactions are so delicate and intricate and different that it's challenging enough to train a good full-time receptionist to be great. Training and re-training and listening to calls to learn how to get better takes time. For these reasons, just the idea that a random receptionist could do this for your firm is borderline insulting.

I realize that answering services come up with a lot of clever responses to the above objections, including what their new technology will do for you. But the only one I've ever experienced who can deliver on these promises costs almost three times as much as a full-time dedicated receptionist anyway!

Clients and potential clients can tell when you've hired an answering service. To think otherwise is silly. Like it or not, a receptionist company makes you seem unprofessional and cheap, like you're not doing well enough to hire someone full-time. That's the reality, even if that company is doing a passable job of merely answering the phone and taking messages.

To a receptionist at a reception company, all calls are equal. But a receptionist that works for you full-time knows the difference between VIP clients and new prospects, between clients who have urgent calls and clients who can be put on hold. Do you want your VIP client being treated like a run-of-the-mill new caller? Of course not.

The VIP client is paying top dollar for premium service, but the answering service makes it sound like you don't know who they are. Do you want that VIP client being put on hold while the reception company unsuccessfully tries to track you down because you forgot to tell them your schedule changed that day? You'll lose this client's trust, and they'll certainly wonder why they're paying you so much money every month.

What about scheduled calls? Think it's annoying for a client to call at a scheduled time, only to be asked the purpose of their call and then wait for you to be tracked down? There is a time and place for an answering service, and that's overflow for your own team and after hours. It's certainly better to hope an answering service gets the job done if three people happen to call at once than to outright miss the call, to be sure. I could go on, but perhaps a client story will finish painting the picture.

"Propelled us to 7-Figure Growth"

In 2018 we lost our receptionist, and I started looking for a replacement. I quickly realized that the volume of calls we were receiving was difficult for an in-office receptionist to manage along with all the other tasks this person was doing. The candidates we interviewed were terrible, from the barista who canceled his interview twice because he had "a funeral he'd forgotten about" to the student who failed to show up at all. I started looking into some of the bigger players for answering services. We'd had a local service that assisted as backup for our phones, but their quality was severely lacking. We learned the meaning of the phrase "you get what you pay for."

The quotes I received from the major answering services when I told them our call volume was somewhere in the neighborhood of $1,300 a month–for just answering our calls! Then I heard about offshore staffing. For the cost of a minimum wage stateside staffer and only a little more than an answering service, I hired a full-time bilingual receptionist. It was a no-brainer.

We've since hired six international staffers: two receptionists, one client intake, one client engagement specialist, one legal assistant, and one marketing specialist.

This team helped propel our growth into a seven-figure firm, and along with our other eleven US-based staffers, are the backbone of our business.

- Vanessa Vasquez, Esq., Vasquez de Lara Law Group

Quick side note - addressing one of Vanessa's points, *you get what you pay for*, the same is true for offshore help. They are the people looking for bargain basement prices for offshore team members. There are also companies whose sole differentiator is on price. But just like here in the US, you get the talent level that you pay for offshore. The reason offshore hiring - or in our case, nearshore hiring because we recruit primarily out of Latin America - makes so much sense in the first place is because of economic arbitrage.

Can you imagine how awkward it would be if your VIP client gets treated like a run-of-the-mill caller by an answering service?

Paying someone the rates we're discussing in this book gives them a *starting* salary of higher than the median average salary for where they live. From there, they can be promoted and earn even more, as many of our clients have done. We occasionally run into or hear about the lawyers looking to find even cheaper talent, perhaps out of the Philippines or other countries.

Remember, quality matters and your people are a reflection of your firm. With the incredible English-speaking talent in Latin America, combined with the cultural and educational similarities, you'd be amazed at the quality of workers we find, waiting for career opportunities with you. Don't shoot for the bottom of the barrel, shoot for the best of the best.

What You Want in a Receptionist

You should look for a receptionist who will make your clients feel at home. This person is a good listener and pleasant to talk to. We've all had those experiences of feeling like we're bothering someone when we call a business—avoid those receptionists at all costs. Your ideal receptionist is smart enough to pick up on social cues and knows when to deviate from the script.

The Power of a Smile

When you smile on the phone, people can feel it on the other side. This leaves the client with an amazing impression of your company. It shows that you have great employees who want to be there.

If you had a receptionist with a grumpy personality, it would make the client think that they're not happy to work for you. But when your client can feel your receptionist smiling through the phone, it sends subconscious signals that your law practice is trustworthy, professional, and cares about helping them. This simple detail will win you clients and build your reputation.

For example, if your receptionist is instructed to tell callers to schedule an appointment, but the client calls in tears, the receptionist should have enough emotional intelligence to know that this might be an urgent matter and it would be insensitive to suggest scheduling an appointment for next week. They need to promise an earlier call back, even if it's not what you told them to do. Someone who always goes by the book, even when it doesn't make sense for the context, is not the best candidate to be a receptionist.

You want someone who is perceptive, good with people, and can handle challenging situations with grace. Law clients often come to you with difficult, sensitive cases, so your receptionist needs to be skilled at talking to people who may be going through a crisis.

Your Receptionist's Duties

What duties is your receptionist in charge of? Here's a quick list to get started, but if your receptionist has extra capacity in the beginning, don't be afraid to get creative:

1. Answering your phones with a smile
2. Taking messages
3. Scheduling call-backs pursuant to your calendar
4. Patching caller through to other departments/people at your firm
5. Placing outbound calls for your scheduled appointments
6. Confirming with scheduled calls the day before and/or day of
7. Handling clients questions that don't need your attention
8. Following up with online inquiries (i.e. following the 5-minute rule)
9. Calling past clients to check in
10. Other research or help when not answering or placing calls

Chapter Recap

Your full-time receptionist is going to relieve your executive assistant from phone duties, allowing your executive assistant to further take more off your plate. With new client calls and online inquiries returned in five minutes, consultations being booked more often because you're losing fewer leads, clients happier and recommending your firm more, and with more help from your executive assistant, you're going to get more cases and more legal work done.

24 Months to Freedom Roadmap

Second Hire: Receptionist

Cost: $1,995/month

Firm Revenues Before Hire: $17,000/month

Firm Revenues After Hire: $22,000/month

Net Gain: $3,005/month

Total Gain: $9,505/month

Hiring and Training Timetable: Months Four and Five

For more information on how to hire a world class bilingual receptionist, a sample weekly scorecard and more, please visit qrco.de/receptionist or scan this QR code now:

CHAPTER 5

Where Will Your New Clients Come From?

You've now made two hires, your current clients are much happier (as are you), the five-minute rule is being followed, and you have real, focused time for your cases unlike ever before. Now you're wondering where your *new* clients will come from…

You're just as busy as ever, even though that time is spent on higher value efforts resulting in much more revenue for your firm. As it stands right now, you're rather profitable, and having a run rate of $300,000 per year with only around half of that in expenses thanks to your offshore hires (trust me, I wish I had known about offshore hiring when I was at this stage) is providing nice breathing room for you and your family for once.

However, cases don't last forever, and you need a steady and consistent flow of new clients to sustain any law firm. And now that you've hired and trained your full-time receptionist so that you're not flushing the golden toilet on a daily basis and ruining those leads (in case you're asking why you shouldn't hire the marketing assistant to get your phone ringing *before* you hire the receptionist), you're ready to invest in some marketing so that you avoid the feast or famine most small businesses suffer through.

Why do so many small businesses fall victim to the feast or famine cycle? Because when you need business, you hustle, market and network. Then you get the work and attack the work. But while you're doing the work, what are you not doing? Hustling, marketing and networking. So new business isn't coming in. You complete the work, need more work, so then you hustle, market and network again. It's a cycle as old as time, and one that few law firms ever truly get through, unfortunately.

The older guy or gal out networking at the local chamber or BNI? They'll be there 10 years from now, because they won't invest in marketing. They'll stick with what they know, afraid to put themselves out there and possibly "fail."

But not you. Because you know that even though you're tasting a bit of success and riding high on your two incredible hires, you want a real business that doesn't rely solely on you, and you need to make the phones ring consistently. That's where marketing comes in. You need to up your marketing game, but where will you find the time?

Managing your marketing on a consistent basis takes a lot of time and effort, but it's a necessary evil, at worst, and a pleasure, at best, to keep a steady stream of clients coming through your door. For many, marketing is a scary thought, even though you know it's imperative. You probably wish you could give your marketing to someone else entirely and have nothing to do with it, but that doesn't work. If there was a marketing abdication company, that company would be a billion-dollar company overnight.

Why does marketing abdication always fail? Your message about the unique service you offer to your clients has to come from you. Nobody else understands why you do family law or bankruptcy law and how your approach is unique and different from other firms. You're the only one who understands that "special something" that would make someone want to hire you over another lawyer. You can't abdicate your marketing to someone who doesn't understand your message the way you do. You'll be disappointed in the results (and that's the best possible outcome).

You can't abdicate your marketing to someone else who doesn't understand your message the way you do.

But you need to free up more of your time. You need people to push that marketing message into the world for you. And let's face it...you're so busy that you're not following through on all the basic marketing tasks you should be doing on a regular basis anyway.

The business cards you collected at the networking event get shoved to the bottom of a drawer. Your social media feeds go stagnant. Your email newsletter was all the rage for three months, but now you're three months behind.

I've also seen so many situations where a firm owner hires a new marketing company, and the marketing company has lots of great ideas for the law firm, but the firm doesn't have anyone to get the marketing done. Or, if you're like a small minority of folks, you have a mental shelf of marketing ideas stacked to the roof that you would implement if you only had the time.

You get motivated for a few months, get a few clients, then the marketing falls off. Truthfully speaking, the impression that on-and-off-again marketing creates on clients and referral sources is worse than if you hadn't done any marketing in the first place. It reeks of desperation. *Ol' so-and-so is back networking and sending emails, he must need clients again,* they think. It's time to get out of that cycle once and for all.

What is a Marketing Assistant?

A marketing assistant is the person who executes your marketing ideas. They won't be the one coming up with the brilliant ideas, but they'll execute the ideas for you so you can continue to focus on the legal work as well as managing your hires. With a good marketing assistant, you can get your message into the world on a consistent basis.

When you hire a good marketing assistant, you can get your message into the world on a consistent basis.

A good marketing assistant can help you convey your mission, vision, core values, and culture to prospective clients. You can't abdicate total control of your marketing to this person—they're not in your brain, so they won't be good at creating your big-picture marketing plan. But they'll be the extra pair of hands that can carry out your vision while you're busy doing legal work.

Unfortunately, there are cheap and underqualified marketing assistants everywhere. If this has affected you in the past, remember, not all VA's are created equally, which I address later in this book. Once you find a fantastic, positive and quality marketing assistant, the best way to use them is to feed them your ideas so they can run with the implementation. You can keep up the consistent marketing required to attract clients, and you've bought back more time that you can use for billable work.

"From $0 to $500,000 + in the First Year"

In 2020 I sold my 15-person brick-and-mortar law firm and started a 100% virtual consulting practice to help other lawyers grow a firm they could sell like I had.

From the beginning, I knew I wanted to operate this business differently. Instead of doing everything myself, I immediately hired virtual assistants through Get Staffed Up. I knew I wanted to scale quickly, so within six months I hired a marketing specialist who had a lot of global experience and a college degree. Given that she worked full time exclusively for me, **we were able to quickly brand my business, go from 0 to 500 subscribers to my own private Facebook group, accumulate fans on other social media platforms, and go from $0 to over $500,000 in the first year.**

I could not have done that without my marketing assistant. The fact that she is located in another country was not a barrier at all. I recommend GSU to my law firm clients who are building value within their firm. **There is nothing more valuable than an effective team.**

- Victoria L. Collier, Esq., Quid Pro Quo Law

As Victoria says, she hired a marketing *assistant*, not manager, coordinator, or chief marketing officer. Those may come later down the road. What you need early on, whether you have a marketing coach or not, is someone who can help you with the marketing you need to get done at a basic level. Even if you have digital marketing vendors for SEO and/or PPC, a full-time marketing assistant will be able to help execute on fundamental marketing activities that you need to do in your local market to be seen as a legitimate player.

Wondering where to begin? Here are the top seven marketing activities you can assign to your first marketing assistant, along with four bonus activities for those of you eager to really get out there:

1. Prepare and send your email newsletter.
2. CRM management & data entry (Anytime you go to a networking event and come back with business cards or new contacts, your marketing assistant should log important details about each person, where you met them, and whether this person is a potential new client or potential referral source - in your CRM).
3. Outreach to book speaking gigs (Research events with your target audience and cold-email/cold-call organizations).
4. Create a schedule of events to focus your networking time.
5. Social media scheduling and posting (Creating simple graphics and posting across multiple platforms several times per week, repurposing your blogs).
6. Capture and report on firm's monthly marketing goals and metrics (leads, consultations scheduled, consultations conducted, conversions and retainer value).
7. Sending links to former clients and current clients for online reviews

Bonus activities:

8. Edit short videos of you speaking for social media posts, your newsletter and email marketing
9. Organize & run your podcast
10. Plan, book and manage/run lunch-and-learn series
11. Basic website updates

Keep in mind that your marketing assistant is not a substitute for expert vendors like your digital ad agency, SEO consultant, and content writer (even AI blogs need serious review). I still do not trust Google ads or SEO to one offshore assistant who, like any other employee, could quit on you at any time. Hopefully you appreciate this honesty - my goal is to help you grow your law firm through staffing the right way. No one person is going to have the skill set to be effective in these areas, so you need to keep using the experts. But your marketing assistant can help coordinate with these vendors for you, and the right one can handle the list of tasks mentioned above.

When you have a good marketing assistant, you only need to spend a few hours a week on marketing. During this time, you'll review last week's content and discuss pros and cons, reflect on your messaging, and plan this week's steps. Concerned that the list of marketing essentials above is only six items long? Managing a social media content calendar across multiple platforms is a full-time job in and of itself, when done correctly.

My law firm's marketing team, for example, has three offshore assistants, an in-house coordinator, and a domestic fractional chief marketing officer. But we started with one assistant and grew from there. There is just so much to learn about what works and doesn't work for your firm that starting small is the best way to go.

It will take your marketing assistant longer to get ramped up than your receptionist and executive assistant. Marketing is just more complicated. It may take months to get your marketing assistant fully onboarded with your messaging and all the ideas you want to execute. As the old saying goes, *50% of marketing works, if I only knew which 50%.* When you have a domestic marketing assistant, every day matters because you're paying them so much. You need to see a return to justify the cost.

With the advent of offshore hiring, you can throw new ideas at the wall every few weeks and see what works. At such a low cost, you're able to absorb marketing misses. I have "brilliant" marketing ideas all the time. Unfortunately, they often don't work. Thankfully I learn fast and cheap, and I'm on to the next one.

The value of consistent marketing

Let's say you get the brilliant idea to start an email newsletter. You send the first one out and it looks great. You send the second one out and it looks great. And then you get busy and forget about the newsletter and it doesn't go out for months...

You had the right instinct—an email newsletter can be effective—but you just don't have the time to follow through.

Unfortunately, the inconsistency of your newsletter, in this case, can actually damage your reputation and make you look unreliable and unorganized.

Having a marketing assistant by your side to keep all of your marketing operating consistently will not only help you attract clients more consistently, simply because you're more visible. It will also give the impression that you're running a solid practice..

Prospective clients will notice consistency, even if only on a subconscious level. If your business consistently puts out quality marketing materials like a newsletter, prospective clients get the impression that you're professional, well-organized, and have resources.

Chapter Recap

Marketing inconsistently and without integrity in design and message is often worse than not marketing at all, unless you're gunning for the lowest end cases such as traffic tickets (I'm not knocking traffic ticket attorneys, by the way. Marketed the right way, these firms can make big bucks). Getting your message out on a consistent basis with just a few hours a week invested of your time will drive leads to your firm and help you avoid the feast of famine cycle so many others fall victim to. This hire will take you towards the end of your first year, where you will overlap with your next hire. Yes, your marketing assistant will be slightly more expensive than the first two hires (we're still talking just over $13/ hour), but they'll be worth every penny. Your marketing assistant should either have special knowledge, really great experience, or a dedicated marketing degree, so by nature they'll come with a higher price tag. You want the best, and you should be excited to pay for the best. Compared to a domestic marketing assistant, it's close to highway robbery anyway.

24 Months to Freedom Roadmap

Third Hire: Marketing Assistant

Cost: $2,295/month

Firm Revenues Before Hire: $22,000/month

Firm Revenues After Hire: $28,500/month

Net Gain: $4,205/month

Total Gain: $13,710/month

Hiring and Training Timetable: Months Six through Nine

For more information on how to hire a top notch bilingual marketing assistant, a sample job description, weekly scorecard and more, please visit qrco.de/marketing-assistant or scan this QR code now:

CHAPTER 6

Fixing the Leaky Bucket

You've got your marketing assistant cranking and more leads are coming in. Now, you need to develop a system for converting clients from the initial point of contact to the paid consultation. Your next hire is an Intake Specialist.

Your intake specialist is not your receptionist. Many attorneys don't understand this difference, or why both are necessary. Please listen to me. **Both. Are. Necessary.**

The intake specialist is the second step to clogging the now infamous golden toilet. Maybe the imagery and analogy are starting to get murky here. I digress… but don't gloss over the critical importance of this chapter. Whereas the executive assistant is the first hire because we need to buy back the most easily replaceable part of your time, the intake specialist is the next most important hire because failing to hire one, or to hire the right one, is where and why most firms stagnate.

Creating the System

Your receptionist is the person who answers the phone. They have great emotional intelligence and act as the client's first point of contact with your practice. The receptionist is like a caretaker—their goal is to make a potential client confident they called the right place and to move them to the next step of the sales process, and to handle all other calls.

Once on the phone with the potential client, the intake specialist's job is threefold - to screen out potential crazies or otherwise clients who don't fit what you're looking for, to save you from having to answer simple questions and convince the caller they don't need to speak to you until the consultation, and to book the prospects who fit what your firm is looking for to a *paid* consultation. We'll cover those duties below, but first, because sales is psychological, let's talk about building authority.

Your intake specialist receives the call from the receptionist and as insignificant as it may seem, that act alone raises the value of the intake specialist in the potential client's mind. The intake specialist knows more about the firm than your receptionist does. They can answer all of the client's questions about the firm. Because they aren't the ones answering the phone, the client perceives them as someone important, someone whose time is valuable. Not as valuable as yours, but more valuable than the receptionist. The right intake specialist is invaluable to your firm, and because they rarely meet clients in person anyway, is perhaps the most natural fit for a virtual/remote team member.

Why is the interplay between the receptionist and intake specialist so important, and why must there be two? Let's use a doctor's office as our primary example.

The medical industry has done a great job of understanding how to orchestrate the sales process effectively. You need to have so much respect and trust in the physician before you agree to pay them to knock you out and cut you open. Putting the doctor behind many layers gives them esteem, even if you never consciously thought about it. It also maximizes the amount of time they are able to use to generate revenue for the practice. By the time you get to talk to the doctor, you've already spoken to two qualified professionals about your problem and how the doctor might be able to help.

Because the doctor's time is prized, the patient is more likely to agree to the "sale" because they regard the doctor as a trusted authority. You want to create that same impression in your law practice.

If you need a brain surgery, and the surgeon answers the phone, would you get brain surgery from that doctor?

Now, let's say the doctor's office messed up any of these elements. If the doctor answered their own phone, you'd be out in a heartbeat. If the receptionist answered the phone but then said "sure, Dr. Smith is right here and would love to speak with you," you'd hang up after the call and never call back. If the receptionist sent you to the next person higher up, but then that person made the doctor seem readily available, you'd start to question the efficacy of that doctor. Finally, if the doctor was super unorganized and didn't make you feel wanted and welcomed after you had agreed to the visit, you'd wonder if you were really at the right place. (I do realize that doctor's offices are actually some of the most poorly run businesses today and many of us keep our doctors despite the poor bedside manner and lack of follow up and care, but for our purposes (a) at least they get the teams and systems right in order to take your money (sales) and (b) if there were more doctors there would be more competition and they'd have to improve. But we don't have that luxury - we have competition, and we must stand out).

Potential clients form the same impressions about your law firm every day. The mistake we usually make is instead of embracing this reality and feeling empowered that you can do something about it, we tell ourselves how great we are and how hard we're working and expect clients to see it from our perspective.

Try cold shopping your own firm someday. You'll probably be horrified and amazed, and upset you didn't do it sooner. So what's the game plan? With the team in place, build the system and close the deal.

"I finally found the long-term solution"

I was having a hard time finding anyone to perform well in the intake specialist role at my law firm. I spent a lot of money on stateside candidates who didn't last. GSU found me a staffer for much less than half the cost that has been fantastic!

I was sick and tired of mediocre employees, especially at the cost here in the states with substandard work ethic. I finally found the long-term solution. My intake specialist has been with me just shy of six months (and my GSU legal assistant just shy of two years!).

- Carrie Schultz, Esq. [MFR] Men's & Father's Rights Divorce Lawyers / Schultz & Associates

Sealing the Deal

Now that you agree you clearly see you need an intake specialist in addition to your receptionist, let's extrapolate on the threefold duties we mentioned above, plus a few bonus responsibilities: screening, saving your time, and following up/sealing the deal.

In terms of the first duty, acting as a screener, the intake specialist is trying to figure out if this person is a good fit for the firm. Is it the right area of law? Does this client seem legitimate? Is the case potentially valuable? Is it a motorcycle accident, but our niche is trucking accidents? Training your intake specialist to screen out bad potential clients and protect your time from wasted consultations is worth every penny. It won't happen overnight, but you'll learn together how to dial it in after trial, error, review and reflection, rinse, repeat, learn, get better.

Your intake specialist follows through on inbound leads and acts as a sales screener.

The second duty comes into play often because many people at large believe they're entitled to your time without paying for it. Maybe they're used to being able to get other attorneys who don't protect their time on the phone, but sometimes potential clients call in and demand to speak to an attorney. Huge red flag. Handling these energy monsters with care is important, because occasionally they'll leave a bad review online. Avoiding these interactions yourself is critical for managing your energy. Your intake specialist should be trained how to politely redirect these inquiries in another direction, or even offer resources available online. For every bad call your intake specialist prevents you from taking, you're saved from aggravation during the call, the energy it takes to recover, and the time it takes to refocus on what you were doing. Your polite-as-ever receptionist isn't likely qualified to handle these items because those callers will demand to speak to someone, and the buck stops with the intake specialist.

The third major duty of the intake specialist is where they really make their money - booking paid consultations. When the right caller calls at the right time, it's energizing for the entire firm. The next big fish is on the line. New clients are the lifeblood of the firm. Resist the temptation to jump on the phone yourself and ruin it by trying to lock up the new case right then and there. You have a sales system, and that system will impress the client a lot more than just you getting on the phone right when they need you.

By making the potential client pay for the consultation at a later date, you're subconsciously teaching the potential client to respect boundaries, that your time is valuable and will cost them money, and that you must be in demand and high worth because you're not desperate enough to drop everything you're doing and get on the phone. I still know far too many lawyers who make this mistake, and it pains me to witness it.

Why You Should Eschew Free Consultations

Early in my career, I gave free consultations. One day, I was excited because I had three consultations. I was desperate for money, and I thought I'd land all three of these clients. It turned out that all three clients were just kicking the tires, looking for free advice, and had no intention of paying for legal services.

At the end of the day, I felt like I'd been kicked in the gut. I'd wasted the whole day and didn't get any clients out of it. After that disappointment, I decided to do paid consultations. It was a total game changer. It filters out the people who just want to waste your time and get free legal advice. You need to reserve your time for paying customers only, and charging for the consultation will set that expectation immediately.

Your intake specialist will have other duties, of course. The intake specialist can send potential clients that aren't right for you to your referral partners. That's right, if you have an intake specialist, you can make referrals without ever picking up the phone. If you make referrals to another law firm, that law firm will likely make referrals back to you because they value your help - especially when you task your intake specialist with tracking referrals sent and following up with attorneys who sent you cases, critical items for growth that you've never had the time to do before.

The last benefit I'll mention for now is follow up, and we certainly saved the best for last. While every law firm is different, depending on urgency and type of law practiced, the statistic goes that it takes seven follow ups before you get a yes or a no from a prospect.

Your intake specialist needs to keep following up until the client gives a clear "yes" or "no." Who has time to follow up seven times with the dozens of referrals and prospects who have reached out to your firm over the past few weeks? Certainly not you. The same goes for a potential client who did engage in a consultation but didn't sign up for your services right away. Following up yourself will create the impression that you're needy. Having your intake specialist follow up will create the impression that you're professional, organized, and that you care.

Follow up is the final nail in the ol' golden toilet - the above-and-beyond your firm will soon do that will set you apart from all others. Prospects simply aren't always ready to commit upon first contact, especially if you practice estate planning, business law or bankruptcy.

A good follow up system, scheduled out with the help of your CRM, consisting of a mix of emails and phone calls, will really keep your coffers full. This is the juncture where your colleagues who used to be your equals won't understand how you're getting so many new cases.

For criminal defense attorneys, you may not call this next hire an intake person or new client coordinator. You may call them something like a criminal case manager. You're trying to build your own authority, and you should create boundaries and make yourself seem in high demand. That's the criminal defense attorney I want. The one who everyone else wants.

Your intake specialist will make you seem very busy, but this case sounds serious and they're gonna do the scared caller a favor and make sure you see them right away anyway, despite how busy you are. By the time they meet with you, you've already done them a favor by moving around other important business to meet with them, and if you haven't read the book Influence yet, I'll spoil it for you - they owe you a favor in return. Case closed.

For personal injury attorneys, when you're smaller you're fighting an uphill battle with bigger PI firms. A bigger firm means more resources to spend on cases and to wow clients. At this juncture you won't be able to outspend them on marketing, but you can outdo them in other ways, primarily customer service. You won't get all the leads yet, but you'll close the ones you do get. Your receptionist and new client coordinator will wow the clients and make their experience feel first class all the way.

Your follow up will be impeccable with videos and graphics and more that show your value. Whatever your message, you utilize your team to hammer it home. You're not charging for consultations, so the intake specialist's job is to get really good at getting the clients you do want in for consultations right away, and with impeccable follow up until they sign, you'll have fewer no shows than ever.

Another handy task that an intake specialist will help you accomplish, much like your marketing coordinator, is to help you get a grasp on your numbers. They'll focus on key sales metrics, while your marketing coordinator can shift to more true marketing metrics. The difference is that marketing drives leads, but once the prospect contacts your firm, the sales process kicks in.

Once you know your conversion rates with a properly functioning sales system and team, you'll need fewer leads, which means less spend, and it'll be easier to create your business plan for growth. Why decide you need 500 leads for 50 new clients when, with a few strategic hires (with whom you spend the time to train), you find out you actually only need 150? Forget about fancy plans until you're a half million dollar law firm. To get there, you need to hustle, hire and train, as we're hopefully showing you in this book.

The Qualities of an Intake Specialist

You do not need a former or professional intake specialist with years of training. Intake specialists can be trained. They could even be a former receptionist that you promote, as long as they have the right skill set.

While the receptionist is more warm, friendly, and accommodating, the intake specialist has to tell people the hard truth. If a client isn't the right fit for the firm, the intake specialist has to communicate this gracefully. The intake specialist manages expectations in a professional way and can't be afraid to quote the consultation fee and take money.

When working with your intake specialist, there are some mistakes you should avoid. You need to give your intake specialist adequate training. You need to review the game film and provide feedback. You should walk your intake specialist through many possible scenarios before they ever speak to a real client.

You need to give clear instructions on who's a great client and who's not, in writing and in an easy to digest format. You want to end up in as few consultations with a potential client who's a bad fit. The way to accomplish this over time is feedback, feedback, feedback. You should debrief with your intake specialist after every consultation, go over notes, and outline the next steps, whether that be to start the onboarding process or to discuss what could have gone better.

The initial responsibilities list for you intake specialist should look like this:

1. Screen out bad prospects
2. Refer incorrect prospects to your referrals courses and keep track
3. Keep your referral partners updated on matters they've sent you
4. Set paid consultations and take the money
5. Follow up with all prospects who are a great fit but didn't sign up for a consultation at least seven times
6. Prep you for each consultation
7. Follow up with all prospects who paid for a consult and are a great fit but didn't sign up after the consultation at least seven times or until they get a "yes" or a "no"
8. Keep track of all calls and prospects in the CRM
9. Create sales reports on a monthly or weekly basis
10. Serve as emergency backup to the receptionist
11. Watch/listen to recordings weekly to learn how to improve conversions
12. Create follow up glide paths and recommend improvements thereto

After reading this chapter and digesting the above duties, you might be thinking that one intake specialist isn't enough. For high price hourly firms, it should be enough for now. For volume based practices that can drive a lot of inexpensive leads, it may not be. Plus, nothing is better than redundancy. Redundancy makes your life better because emergencies become non-emergencies when you have extra hands on deck. For now though, let's focus on hiring one great intake specialist who will take your firm to the next level.

Bonus Tip: Internationally Speaking, Where You Hire From Matters

One thing I've confirmed since starting with international staffing in 2018 is that there are smart, talented people all over the world. But not all educational systems are created equally. Certain parts of the world have better English programs, resulting in better reading, writing and comprehension. Certain countries have the best infrastructure. Time zone also matters.

Additionally, some countries are so saturated with VA companies that unless you're headhunting (hiring away entrenched employees already employed by another business for a lot of money), you're left with the bottom 20% of qualified people they can find for you. This is a big part of the reason it takes on average seven hires to find the right assistant when you're doing it yourself, and why the company's reach and influence with whom you work is so critical. The "DIY" method of hiring is really tough, and so is working with the wrong company with the wrong strategy.

For more on why we hire exclusively from the dynamic workforce in Latin America, instead of from the Philippines, India, or any other traditional VA hub like most offshore staffing companies do, please see my video below.

https://qrco.de/notallvasarethesame

To be clear, your intake specialist and your executive assistant should also be two different people. You need detailed notes from each consultation. Do you know how frustrating it is for a potential client when you can't have a good conversation because you're typing notes? Or how hard it is on every team member down the line because your notes from the consultation are porous? Your executive assistant or legal assistant (stay tuned!) should be taking notes during consultations while you give undivided attention to the client.

Though it is a sales position, your intake specialist should not be salesy and doesn't need sales experience. When you truly believe in what you're selling, it's not a sale at all. Your intake specialist just has to understand your practice and what kinds of clients you can serve. That way, they can tell the clients, "You've come to the right place, we can help you," and it comes from the heart. That doesn't require 20 years of sales experience.

Chapter Recap

Hiring an intake specialist will take your consultation setting to another level. You'll become more picky with cases because thanks to your small but steady flow of leads, adherence to the five-minute rule, and your intake specialist setting up consultations without you, you've reversed the golden toilet phenomenon and have your pick of the litter.

You'll get better cases and healthier clients, which will have a ripple effect on your firm (not the least of which is your profit, which now has the profound effect of reducing your stress, making your personal life and family much happier, and making you a better lawyer - and person - to be around).

With all the consultations and new cases, you'll begin to wonder who will help with the legal work, as growth brings new challenges. This hire will take you into year two, with more precise training and review necessary. With four full-time hires, including an intake specialist to help with the initial part of the sales cycle, you're starting to leave the *Hustle* stage and enter the *Experiment* stage, with few but precious moments to start working on your business.

24 Months to Freedom Roadmap

Fourth Hire: Intake Specialist

Cost: $2,145/month

Firm Revenues Before Hire: $28,500/month

Firm Revenues After Hire: $35,500/month

Net Gain: $4,855/month

Total Gain: $18,565/month

Hiring and Training Timetable: Months Ten through Thirteen

For more information on how to hire a top quality Intake Specialist, a sample job description, weekly scorecard and more, please visit qrco.de/intake-specialist or scan this QR code now:

CHAPTER 7

The Bane of Your Existence: Billing

Let's be clear… No lawyer likes billing, and even fewer of us like preparing, perfecting, and sending invoices. For reasons I've never truly understood, it's the bane of our existence, and yet the biggest factor holding us back financially. Our next step is to hire someone who will remove this tremendous burden from you that is silently killing your productivity and cash flow—a virtual billing assistant.

Small firm attorneys are notorious for not invoicing for their work. I know attorneys who have hundreds of thousands of dollars in work to invoice, but they just don't send the bills.

The problem is caused by not: (a) accurately capturing your time, (b) preparing succinct yet informative invoices that clients want to pay, (c) sending the actual invoices out, and then (d) collecting the money goes so deep it actually hurts to write about. But we must go there - because you have to understand just how bad the problem is, how straightforward it is to actually fix, and what fixing the problem will do for your cash flow, your bank account, and your sanity.

I've been there, and I feel bad for my former self for the way I used to handle billing. I tried hiring a local billing clerk ten or so years ago who was supposed to come in on Saturdays. (Yes, I thought it would be cheaper this way, and I got what I tried to pay for. As I said, I've been there, so I'm in no position to criticize anyone. But I am now in a unique position to help.)

The first few Saturdays were mired in confusion as I had trouble fully explaining all of the cases that I thought my super part-timer should be able to pick up on quickly. Then she missed a few Saturdays. Then we made some progress. Then she probably decided that doing anything else on her Saturdays was way cooler than spending a portion of her weekend trying to help save the mess I was creating all week, so she politely quit.

Sound familiar?

I bet 90% of us have been there - and less than that percentage can admit we're creating our own misery through our mindset and actions.

The Major Challenges with Billing

Let's tackle the four main issues in chronological order, each of which cascades upon the other to create a big heaping pile of.... And let's give you easy solutions for now, just to get started. These are the quick and easy fixes - just take action now and improve later.

Challenge #1

The first issue is that very few of us capture our time correctly in the very first instance. I'll never forget at the law firm I first worked for after law school, the owner would look at his account, realize he needed money, tell his too-qualified-to-do-timekeeping paralegal to pull up a word doc and type, while he started listing the pleadings, motions and other actions he had taken on the case over the prior few weeks, all to the best of his memory.

The result was that the law firm owner would decide he deserved a certain amount for all his work, and backtrack his way there. Even as a young lawyer who knew almost nothing, I thought this was a terrible way to go about business. He would also burn through the retainer in a few days without warning then, without providing any time records, ask for more money.

This resulted in a lot of unhappy clients and former clients. It was unfair to the clients, unfair to the staff, and unfair to the firm itself.

But he's not alone, not hardly. Very few lawyers capture time as they work. While capturing time isn't fun, not doing so isn't fair to the client or the firm because it's inaccurate.

If You're a PI Attorney You Need This Role Instead...

Personal injury attorneys likely don't need a billing assistant, you need a medical records clerk.

A full-time medical records clerk can be a game changer, instead of trying to work with an outside vendor or doing it yourself. Imagine how much time you'd save if you had a full-time medical records clerk? You can hire one for less than $2,000 a month.

Attorneys who wait until the end of the day to capture their time - when they do remember before shutting it down for the day - end up losing 10% to 15% of their time. Attorneys who wait until the end of the week lose 20% to 30% of their time. Why?

May I shout it from the roof one more time - you don't realize how much all the small things add up! Just as you don't realize how scheduling your own calls and appointments accumulates to loads of time, you forget about the little actions you took on a case, some of the research, the phone calls, and even how long some of the emails took you to write, so you don't bill for them.

Even if your firm doesn't charge for some of those items, you should track them. The only reason not to track your time is because the truth scares you, which is a terrible reason not to track your time. You could pay someone to follow you around all hours of the day and track your time and they would pay for themselves.

This is another huge factor in why solo and small firm lawyers only collect on average 1.2 hours per day - we work on the cases more than that, but lose the time because it isn't tracked correctly, so we're probably working about two hours just to bill 1.2.

Solution #1

Keep a secure spreadsheet on Google Sheets, and do the most simple time capture as you go throughout your day. Then, each following morning, your virtual billing assistant takes the entries from the spreadsheet and puts them into your time keeping software in a more robust and thorough manner that you will teach them. As stated, I also hated billing for my time when I did legal work at my law firm, and this method competently got me through many years of growth until we had a bigger team and developed new methods.

Stopping what you're doing to bring up your case management software, enter the matter name, input the time and wordsmith the action each and every time you switch tasks is a productivity killer and adds to your hesitancy to capture your work in the most accurate way.

On that spreadsheet that is shared with your billing assistant, you only need a few columns - the matter name, brief description, and amount of time. Leave the sheet open on your computer so it's easy to access, enter those three items with an abbreviated description, and that's it. You've done your job, and you'll teach your virtual billing assistant to take it from there.

Challenge #2

Preparing invoices stinks. There's no way around it. I still have nightmares about hitting the batch pre-bill button, only to have 30 invoices about 4-5 pages long each to go through and correct. *This client likes everything separated, this client likes the time entries batched, this client complains every time, and this little client went wee-wee-wee allll the way home.*

I think, much like my Saturday billing clerk back in the day, we'd almost rather do anything else. Unfortunately, most of the time, that's exactly what we do. Anything else.

The bad news is that in order to get paid, unless you're a contingency or flat-fee fee firm, the billing must be done. The better you word your time entries, to fully explain why each item was necessary, the more likely you get paid without complaints. For most attorneys, billing becomes weekend or late-night work. You run out of time to handle it during working hours, so you end up doing it exhausted on the couch while Netflix is playing instead of spending time with your loved ones.

While this may be fun when you first start your firm and feel like a rite of passage, it's just not sustainable. The great news is that like almost everything else you don't love to do in your firm, this, too, can be delegated. Your sanity depends on it.

Solution #2

You guessed it - teaching your virtual billing assistant how to do the time entries. One of the reasons why delegation can sometimes be a dirty word (although it shouldn't be) is because if we delegate something we don't like doing, we feel bad because we assume the employee to whom we delegate doesn't like those tasks either.

First, never assume. Second, you're going to hire someone who actually likes numbers and billing and wants to do these tasks for you. You're going to think they're crazy for liking this role, they're going to think you're crazy for being a lawyer, and you're going to get along swimmingly.

The devil is in the details here, to be sure. You have to teach your virtual billing assistant how to word your invoices by creating four to five types of wording samples per entry type. This way they can learn to take what you've written on the shared and private spreadsheet and enter the time in a way that is written just like you want them to be written.

Painful at first, sure. But less painful than doing it yourself after a few months (because there will be a lot of discussions, reflection and learning early on), and less painful every month thereafter, until you're jumping for joy at the progress. I'm also happy to mention at this point that - if the solutions I've outlined so far don't align with how you envision running your billing department - there are lots of companies who can teach you great systems, and we're happy to refer them to you.

Challenge #3

Sending invoices out is less of a challenge these days because software continues to get better. Some of you have client portals or automatic emails, and it seems to get you by. Most of us don't, however, and we're certainly not sending out invoices on a regular basis because they were never properly prepared in the first place. So if you're thinking you don't need a billing assistant because you use Clio, for example, I hate to break it to you but Clio isn't a magic wand.

So what happens is that because we take months and months to get our acts together and send invoices, which we're only doing because we've put ourselves, and our bank accounts, in dire situations, we look at the total amount on the invoices and we feel bad.

Instead of feeling great for ourselves for how much legitimate time and effort we put into the matter, we feel terrible because we waited so long and now the bill is large. We impute our own feelings about money and where we stand in business, and we can't imagine having to pay a bill that size ourselves.

We all do this.

Instead of focusing on how much better we're making our clients' lives, we stare at that total bill and wonder if we're going to make them upset.

So what do we end up doing? Discounting the invoices, sometimes significantly. Remember how we're so busy burning the midnight oil and doing everything ourselves, and we're not capturing all of our time in the first place, so we can barely bill 2 hours per day when we're on our own?

Now we're discounting the amount again, and that's how we end up collecting a mere 1.2 hours worth of legal work per day. It starts to really get you in the pit of your stomach when you fully bring it to light. Maybe that's why we avoid billing so much - it's easier to just ignore the pain and focus on the work and the next case while the mess we've created continues to grow.

I know attorneys who have hundreds of thousands of dollars in work to invoice, but they just send the bills.

To compound the issue even further, clients hate getting sporadic invoices. *Why didn't you bill me for five months, mr. attorney? And now I got this huge bill? My lawyer must need to pay bills because I finally got an invoice.*

These are all thoughts our clients have when we can't do the simple and professional task of sending bills on a consistent basis. So not only are you billing them for less than an hour a day, your clients aren't even happy to pay you for this discounted time. And why should they be? It's not their fault, and they don't even know you're already billing them for so much less than the amount of time you've worked.

Solution #3

Lo and behold, a billing assistant. Again, even if you have decent software, you shouldn't be the one hitting the send button. Further, most invoices require at least some formatting and other actions to get them out. This is really low hanging fruit for a billing assistant, whereas challenges numbers one and two above were the heaving lifting.

Let's get you on schedule, and help your billing assistant manage their weeks. Take your client list, and divide them up into quarters. One easy way is by last name - A through G, H through M, N through S, and T through Z, or any other method which is easy to follow that you choose. On four week cycles, your billing assistant is preparing pre-bills, reviewing time entries, sitting with you for only an hour at the same time every week to force you to review them on time, making any changes and corrections, then sending out the invoices.

What used to take you 10 hours now takes two. This system is scalable, provides for weekly cash flow, and gets your firm - and clients - on a steady rhythm of work out, money in. As the Mandalorian would say, this is the way.

Challenge #4

Ever have to chase a client down for money?

This is the final straw in the camel's back for why lawyers hate billing so much. It's not fun asking for money. You want clients to pay you without having to ask. Then there are always the ones who complain. Sometimes there is a legitimate reason, such as a billing entry got messed up.

Instead of losing your cool and becoming frustrated, realize that small mistakes are actually an opportunity to showcase how you react to adversity and, if handled the right way, will make you stand out more than if the mistake had never happened. (This is a life truism, by the way. Use adversity to create stickiness and convince people you're someone they love to do business with).

Then there are the ones who complain that the invoice is three times larger than it should have been because you waited so long to send it, and they're right. So you feel bad and offer another discount to appease them. By this time, you're lucky if you collect half of what you actually should have billed for.

Finally, there are the clients who complain just to complain. This is the final reason you must separate yourself from the process. There's so much guilt surrounding something that should be very transactional. You do work at an agreed upon price, you get paid. It should be that simple, and yet it rarely is.

Solution #4

As always, it comes back to your team. In this case, the billing assistant who is going to organize the colossal mess in a few short months. By acting as the layer between you and the client, and asking for the money from the clients who don't pay when they get the invoice, they're going to be a buffer between you and the frustration.

Hate having the money conversation with a client? Don't have it. You'll start to tell real quickly who your good clients are. Good clients will appreciate consistent sounding invoices that are clear and sent on time every month. Bad clients love it when you get behind, waiting to pounce on your guilt for yet another discount. Let your billing assistant handle these tasks for you. It's not personal, it's just business. You need to get paid.

You're also their lawyer, so you don't need to be the one sending them emails asking for money. If it's left up to you, you likely won't do it. But a billing assistant will. It's their job, and you can even incentivize them to do it well.

Let's Dive Into Some Numbers

Not totally convinced because your firm is different and the solutions above won't work for you? Let's dive into some numbers, since we are talking about billing, after all. Even when you do get around to sending your invoices, every time you handle your own billing, you're losing money.

Each and every facet of the billing process are examples of those $10 an hour tasks we were talking about earlier, costing you $50 every 10 minutes.

Every time an attorney handles their own billing, they lose money, and much more than they think.

But now that you have a billing assistant, you'll collect more of what you've already worked for because you now have a reliable system to account for what your clients owe you. You'll make more money on top because you'll have even more time to get additional legal work completed.

A billing assistant who systematizes your billing and invoicing and gets them to clients on a consistent date each month will increase your bottom line by 15% - 25%. The return on a billing assistant can be measured dollar for dollar with some basic accounting.

Calculate your collection rate for the past 12 rolling months, hire a virtual billing assistant, train them properly, and then calculate that same rate. Compared to what a full-time virtual billing assistant will cost you in dollars alone, you'll wonder why you ever operated for a single day without one.

If you take away just two things from this book (and I certainly hope it's more), it should be this: you need an executive assistant to protect your time, and you're losing gobs and gobs of money by not having one. Again, it would be like running a restaurant without a cashier and sending your diners a bill at an unspecified later date.

You earned it, now collect your darn money.

You'll be happier, and so will your family and clients. When you add in the hours of your life you'll get back from this hire, it's hard to argue there's a better hire pound for pound.

Do you need this person full-time? Yes, you do. I can hear you subconsciously fighting me and making excuses while I write this, convincing yourself you can save a few extra bucks with a part-time billing assistant. In fact, you're a lot closer to needing a second billing assistant than you are to needing one only part-time, you just don't realize it yet.

Your billing assistant should enter your time every day, send invoices to 25% of your clients every week, and then follow up and collect. They will be plenty busy, especially with your new-found 10 to 20 hours a month and increased productivity.

Speaking of proper training, you know who can help you train this person? Your executive assistant you hired back in month one and trained to do some of the billing because it's one of the first things, after your email and your calendar, you took off your plate. See how things get easier as you grow and get more help? That's what we're here for.

You know what else your billing assistant can do for you? Something that will pay for themselves tenfold in just a few months - attack your A/R.

"We went from a 65% collection rate to over 95% in 2 months"

We had a big problem within our law firm. Revenues were good but collecting it had become a major issue. We had over $160,000 in accounts receivable and several clients who were past due more than 90 days. It was a mess. My office manager, who did not have a background in accounting, was seriously overwhelmed in trying to tackle the problem.

We contacted GSU and were quickly paired with Natalia. She had a stellar background working for a mid-size CPA firm in Argentina as an accountant for the last six years.

We got Natalia Quickbooks training and my firm admin spent some time teaching her how to use our billing software and its idiosyncrasies.

Natalia was a fast learner and within two weeks had mastered everything we could have asked her to in our system. From there, we created the billing team with my firm administrator, my office manager, and Natalia.

My office manager was responsible for collection calls, the firm administrator was to deal with escalations, and Natalia ran the software and was the glue holding it all together.

Natalia organized the billing team and reduced our open accounts receivable by $120,000 in two months, and we went from about a 65% collection rate to over 95%.

Fast forward to this year: Natalia not only handles our billing, but she handles all of our accounting and financial reporting and they have created a reporting schedule to keep reporting coming to me on a consistent basis.

Natalia may be from Argentina but at a fraction of the cost of a US-based accountant she would probably run circles around all of them.

- Sam Brotman, Esq., Brotman Law

As I said at the beginning of this chapter, I know plenty of attorneys with hundreds of thousands of dollars in accounts receivable (or, more accurately, in unbilled work). I'm appreciative of Sam for being honest and sharing. What Sam then did was take the concept and go to the next level. He didn't collect some A/R and then fire the staffer, hoping to save a few bucks. He realized the concept worked, so he built on it.

Sam's experience of adding highly talented virtual staffers to his team, which led to the creation of a completely independent finance department in which he doesn't sit, isn't unique. It's a smarter and more financially responsible way to staff, and if you stick with it and continue betting on yourself, you'll find it's easier than you think.

The Qualities of a Billing Assistant

Your billing assistant should be decent with numbers, first and foremost. They also need to be good at writing, and be very organized. They need to be able to press a client for payment, so you don't want a billing assistant who is the sweetest person on the block like your receptionist. They should also be able to communicate with clients without being offensive, insensitive, or sounding too robotic. This person should have a lot of balance and not be too excitable or emotional.

The job duties of your billing assistant are straightforward and should look like this:

1. Add attorney time entries into billing software.
2. Create time entries pursuant to firm's guidelines.
3. Run pre-bills and sit with the firm owner/manager every Wednesday to review.
4. Make corrections to pre-bills and run invoices.
5. Send invoices to clients.
6. Collect monies due from clients.
7. Track work in progress and flag attorneys when matters exceed $5,000 so the firm can send intermediate bills to clients and keep them happy.
8. Provide basic financial reporting with help of software.
9. Collect accounts receivable.
10. Handle initial clients queries and escalate when necessary.

Chapter Recap

For unknown reasons, lawyers hate billing more than anything, and we avoid it like the plague. Your billing assistant will take this burden off of you, and by getting your bills out the same time every month, you'll see cash flow start to improve and be semi-predictable for the first time. This hire will take more hands-on training, and you'll need to be more involved in the early stages than with the other hires, but your AR will vastly improve, and the amount of hours you write-off on your invoices will dwindle. You'll wonder why you didn't make this move sooner, as you're trading pennies for dollars once again. This hire will put you on the fast track to becoming a firm that other lawyers want to work for, which conservations you'll start to have soon, as you're now about a half million dollar law firm. But your plate is still full, and you're anxious to make the next hires very soon.

24 Months to Freedom Roadmap

Fifth Hire: Billing Assistant

Cost: $2,295/month

Firm Revenues Before Hire: $35,500/month

Firm Revenues After Hire: $43,500/month (plus lots of AR collected)

Net Gain: $5,705/month

Total Gain: $24,270/month

Hiring and Training Timetable: Months Fourteen through Seventeen

For more information on how to hire a top quality billing assistant, a sample job description, weekly scorecard and more, please visit qrco.de/thebillingassistant or scan this QR code now:

CHAPTER 8

Let's Get Legal

At this point, if everything has gone well, you're desperately ready to start delegating some of your legal work. Your executive assistant is probably going to be your de facto legal assistant for a while, as we previously mentioned they'll handle many items for you when they first start. They'll handle your emails and correspond with opposing counsel on your behalf, and potentially do some e-filing or other related tasks for you.

This works well for a while, but you're going to reach a breaking point where you need a legal assistant. You have a marketing assistant and an intake specialist now. Both of these people are doing their jobs well, and it's bringing in a growing flow of clients. Your executive assistant is swamped with what they already have, and they can't take on anything else. Your billing assistant is making sure the money is coming in, so you get paid more for the work you're already doing.

You've freed your time so that you're doing much more legal work, and your revenue has grown. It's getting to the point where you have more clients than you can handle, even when you're spending all day on billable work.

Bonus Point: An Important Note on Turnover

While managing virtual team members is easier than you think when you put in the effort, it does take work. As does all leadership/management of employees.

Have you ever been burned when hiring in-house? Of course you have. We all have. The offshore world isn't perfect, either.

Because we hire only the top 1% of the thousands of offshore applicants who we have vetted, tested, put through a weeks-long screening process and then a test-flight academy, our success rate is much higher than the average hiring success rate in the U.S.

We do have the occasional client who hires a virtual assistant and gives them a project while only periodically checking in, without giving clear instructions, timelines, and most importantly, feedback. This is a recipe for failure.

Turnover does happen though, and it's important to move on quickly when you know you don't have the right fit. But you can only do that by giving constant feedback, training, and checking in, especially for the first 4-8 weeks. And when you work with a team like ours who replaces your staffer within days to a week, on average, your loss of momentum is greatly minimized.

There's a reason it takes about 24 months to get to freedom, not 24 days. You must train your team. There are no exceptions. Owning *your* responsibility for *your* team makes all the difference.

You need to start bringing in legal help or you're going to be in trouble. You don't want to hold back your growth because you don't have the capacity for more clients. And if you try to get by with the employees you have, it will show in the quality of your work, and your clients will know that you're overburdened.

You don't want to hold back your growth because you don't have the capacity for more clients.

Your legal assistant can take some work off your plate. They can set court dates, coordinate the court calendar, do e-filing and service, manage client communication, organize and keep client files, monitor deadlines, set court, mediation and hearing dates, and provide client updates. They can also take notes during consultations, and should help with client onboarding. If you're a flat-fee firm, the legal assistant can learn how to do some form drafting and gathering of documents you need from the clients.

A lot of lawyers have difficulty delegating legal work. We all think that we're the best lawyer in the world, and that allowing someone else to help will weaken our product. That might be true if you have abdicated all of your work to someone else, but if you have systems in place so that everything ready to be filed or shared is given to you in an electronic folder the day before, you can take 20-30 minutes to look at it and be done with it. Maybe not at first, but as your legal assistant gets better, more time gets added back to your plate.

You need relief with this tedious and repetitive work so you can do the high-level analysis and drafting that requires your expert touch. This is how you'll be able to take on more clients and bring in more revenue without overworking yourself.

Delegate with Confidence

Let's get over your fear of delegating basic legal work, because this is where so many lawyers get hung up. I used to spend countless hours editing my own pleadings, playing with margins and fonts, learning email service rules, etc. I found it so much more enjoyable than billing, that's for sure. This is where I "hid out" and wasted a lot of hours. So even if you *don't mind* this type of work, like me, it's holding you back. The number one asset of every firm is the time of the owner, and that time needs to be used wisely.

The best way to ensure that you feel completely confident handing work to someone else is to create detailed checklists. Once created, your legal assistant now has a checklist holding them accountable to your process, so you don't have to worry that they'll forget a step or file something the wrong way. Delegation by oral direction, bad. Delegation in clear writing, good. I should say it louder for the people like me who lack patience and who at times fail to reduce instructions to writing.

If you take the time to develop and record standardized procedures, training a legal assistant becomes painless. You can start handing off all of the annoying, time-consuming tasks that used to slow you down, and even though you might not have hated the work, it's incredibly freeing.

We put the legal assistant late in the hiring process for a reason. Unlike some of your other roles, this hire requires specific training focused on your unique firm. It's a luxury to have the rest of your support team in place so you have time to train the legal assistant the right way. Getting caught up in these tasks doesn't drain your energy as much as the administrative or billing duties, so they can be delegated later. But with the legal assistant, we're talking about working on the actual deliverables of your firm.

The way you run your production is different from others. Your bankruptcy, estate planning, or family law firm likes to perform a certain way. Tweaking the legal procedures is usually in your wheelhouse, and most of the training should come from you, at least until you're a *Systemizer* or *Influencer*.

You'll have a better grasp on the legal assistant's tasks early on than you would perhaps the intake specialist. This is the first step to getting out of the legal production in your firm, so dive in with two feet realizing that you'll be there as a mentor and supervisor every step of the way.

Virtual or In-House?

Some assume it's not possible to use a virtual team member for this position. I work with attorneys who use virtual legal assistants all the time, and it's possible to get fantastic results with a remote hire. I will say that if you want to spend the money to have one in-house, domestic hire in your small firm, this would be it. If you had to choose one, it would be preferable to have the legal assistant in-house than the executive assistant or receptionist.

Your executive assistant organizes you and your life, your legal assistant touches and organizes the work, which is more suited for a hands-on position between the two.

You also might appreciate having someone else in the office to keep you company and be present for in-person consultations. Other than that, there's not much you lose in opting for a virtual legal assistant.

I've long maintained that having a robust offshore virtual team will help you make more and better hires domestically. So if you're worried about not providing jobs here in the U.S., rest assured that if you don't grow, you won't provide *any* jobs for anyone, anywhere. I believe the local hires you should make should be attorneys and paralegals, with the rest of your team offshore in order to keep costs down. But if you're keen on providing jobs locally like many of us, understand that the more financially stable your firm is, the more job security you can provide.

If you have or desire a 100% remote law firm like many of our clients, kudos to you. If you'd like a hybrid workforce like so many others, you'll be pleasantly surprised at how international team members with exceptional English from Latin America share most of our culture and add such vibrancy and energy to your firm.

The main advantage to hiring a virtual legal assistant is that you save so much money in overhead costs. Unless you work with a lot of paper files, there's not a quality difference between virtual and in-house legal secretaries. Almost 100% of legal assistant work is over the phone or through the computer when you really break it down. Your virtual employee saves time by not having to commute, and you both skip the distractions that can come with working in-office with another person.

Bonus Tip: It's Easier Than You Think to Create a Thriving Virtual Culture

One objection people invest when objecting to hiring virtually - without really ever putting much thought into it - is that it's tough to manage virtual team members.

Nonsense.

It takes effort, like anything else. People who are good employers, care about their team, have standards and enforce them in a fair and consistent fashion, and motivate their team to strive for greatness can manage a team who is next door or the next continent over.

It's easier than you think. Visit this site for a value-packed guide on events and many other fun and productive ways you can create a fantastic work environment for your virtual team:

https://www.getstaffedup.com/thrivingvirtually

We had a client early on who hired a staffer from us. This client was a lawyer who was known for being disorganized. The staffer we found for her was so good that in a short amount of time, her colleagues began asking her how she got her act together almost overnight.

Finally, she was meeting her deadlines, corresponding in a more timely fashion, and filing better motions. For unfortunate reasons, the attorney ended up letting the staffer go.

We had heard the stories of how capable this legal assistant was, so we ended up bringing her in-house, and after many promotions she's currently a Director and runs a 10-person department in our company. She's so talented that we helped sponsor her move from Mexico to the U.S. because that was her dream, which she was upfront about from day one.

This employee of ours single-handedly got our client so organized that her colleagues were shocked and wanted to know her secrets. She's not the only example. There are some stellar legal assistants in the virtual workforce who can help turn your practice around if you give it a chance.

Finally, because at this point you're now on your sixth offshore hire, and your firm is growing like wildfire, I can discuss a high level concept with you. I've long said that a paralegal is the toughest position to staff at a law firm.

Hiring several offshore legal assistants and promoting the best ones to paralegal is another brilliant move that has been made by many of our clients. Think about the economics involved here - you pay your offshore staffer, who has been trained as a legal assistant for a year or two and promoted to a paralegal, around $500 to $550 a week. You require her to bill 15 hours per week (on the low end), and you bill her at $200 an hour. She'll be netting you around $2,500 a week and $10,000 a month. You're trading pennies for dollars.

Before we get ahead of ourselves too much, let me assure you that excellent paralegals don't fall off trees, even in the United States. We've researched adding paralegals to our offerings, but if you've ever hired someone with a paralegal certificate and no experience, you know they still need lots of training. So stick with the game plan for now, hire one legal assistant, train them up, and never look back.

"Our legal assistant has been absolutely fantastic"

When I founded my firm I performed every single job function in the firm.

As more work started to flow into the firm, my job became increasingly more difficult because I was doing everything on my own.

I was having lunch with one of my clients and commented on how great her assistant was in terms of scheduling our meetings and handling other administrative tasks. She shared with me that she found her assistant through GSU and recommended that I look into doing the same.

I took her advice and, shortly thereafter, hired my legal assistant through GSU.

Our legal assistant has been absolutely fantastic and is an integral part of the work we do. There are now four attorneys with the firm and she supports all of us in so many ways.

- Chris Lomax, Esq., Lomax Legal PLLC

The Qualities of a Legal Assistant

Your legal assistant needs to be extremely organized. They'll be in charge of your deadlines when you turn the reins over, and while you should have backup systems and ticklers so you don't miss something, you'd like your legal assistant to be rigid to appoint or always trying to keep you on task. They will communicate with clients, so some bedside manner is also a requirement. Because you'll be spending a decent amount of time with this person, as long as you're an okay person to be around, they should be, too.

Your legal assistant's duties will vary based on your type of law firm, but here are some initial ideas:

1. Preparing, editing and finalizing e-filing and e-service pursuant to firm checklists.
2. Drafting, editing and finalizing client correspondence.
3. Securing and setting court dates and communicating with JA's.
4. Organize client files.
5. Maintain firm's legal calendar and monitor deadlines.
6. Provide client case updates after hearings of major events.
7. Help prepare you or other firms lawyers for hearings and client meetings.
8. Scheduling depositions, mediations and hearings.
9. Taking notes during consultations.
10. Opening files and assisting with new client onboarding.

Chapter Recap

With the legal matters piling up, you need some relief. You're at your wits end with legal work up to your eyeballs, and your executive assistant is begging you to get help on the legal side. Hiring a legal assistant to take the mundane but critical tasks off yours, and your executive assistant's plates, saves you from misery. You wanted to grow your firm, but each new level brings a new devil.

The legal assistant needs hand-holding as they're learning new tasks never before performed, but because of their great attitude, intellect, and willingness to learn, they pick it up quickly. After a few months, you're ready to hand the reins off to the legal assistant, saving you from the excruciating tasks of e-filing, service, client updates, and more. Training is more tedious and focused than the rest, but your executive assistant helps, and you're wondering how you ever ran a law firm without these resources in the first place.

24 Months to freedom Roadmap

Sixth Hire: Legal Assistant

Cost: $2,145/month

Firm Revenues Before Hire: $43,500/month

Firm Revenues After Hire: $47,000/month

Net Gain: $1,355/month (but much needed sanity and head space)

Total Gain: $25,625/month

Hiring and Training Timetable: Months Eighteen through Twenty

For more information on how to hire a top quality legal assistant, a sample job description, weekly scorecard and more, please visit qrco.de/legal-assistant or scan this QR code now:

CHAPTER 9

You Have More Clients, Now Let's Keep Them Happy!

At this juncture you've got a great team in place, and can't believe how far you've come. You barely recognize your firm compared to when you started. You're doing good legal work, getting referrals, bringing a stream of clients through marketing, and getting paid.

Now we need to keep these clients happy so they stay loyal and refer you to their network. We're going to bring in a client engagement specialist — also known as a client happiness coordinator.

Like an account manager, the client happiness coordinator is in charge of making the clients feel loved. Your legal assistant has handled much of this client interaction until now, but the legal assistant doesn't have the time to give your clients the level of personal interaction that leads to excellent referrals. This person will also take over reviews and testimonials from your marketing assistant as they'll know your clients better than anyone.

Your ideal client happiness coordinator is someone with fantastic social abilities. They're outgoing, pleasant, and friendly. They aren't just good at talking to clients—they look forward to it. They make each client feel special and cared for.

What A Client Happiness Coordinator Can Do

Imagine if each time you called the doctor's office, you spoke to someone who knew your name and history and could help you with anything: retrieving medical records, answering questions, and making recommendations and referrals. They know the names of your kids and remember their last visit. You would never go anywhere else, and you would tell everyone you knew how great the service was. You trust this doctor because they have a person whose whole job is to take care of you and make sure you have a great customer experience. This doctor really cares about you–not just your money.

When done right, a client happiness coordinator gives the same effect in a law firm. Your clients will feel like you care about them, and it'll keep them loyal to your firm. The best part is that you don't have to put in any of the time it takes to create this personalized customer experience.

Your client happiness coordinator should call your clients on a regular basis. These calls are just for the purpose of checking in and seeing if the client needs help with anything.

Maybe your client needs recommendations on where to get a new car, and you happen to know the owner of the dealership. Maybe it's the week of the deposition, and the happiness coordinator sends the client a video on depositions and goes over key points.

On these calls, your happiness coordinator can make sure your client is feeling calm about each step of the legal process and ease some of their anxieties.

One personal touch I really like is asking the clients about their favorite meal the night before a deposition or mediation. You can have the meal delivered the next day, and the client will feel special. Ever had a good deposition or mediation turn sour because your client got hungry? No longer happens at your firm.

Your client happiness coordinator can call former clients, too. On these calls, you're not explicitly asking for referrals. You're just checking in to ask how they're doing. Usually, this leads to referrals because it reminds them about your business.

The client happiness coordinator executes your high-touch client "wow" process. This could include sending client onboarding packages via email or mail when a client hires your firm. Most firms do this through a paralegal, but if you have someone trained to curate the experience, it'll change the way your firm is perceived.

The client happiness coordinator is probably more friendly by nature than your average paralegal, who might be a more technical person. Creating a truly personal client experience takes time that your paralegal doesn't have. When you designate a client happiness coordinator, this person can spend more time getting the details right and personalizing each interaction.

Speaking of Client Happiness Coordinators and What They Can Help You Build...

Want to join our Facebook Community called *Liberated Lawyer Lifestyle* (or L3, for short)?

In this community we post tips, hold discussions, and invite discourse on getting off the hamster wheel hustle and delegating our way to freedom.

If you'd like to interact with other like-minded layers in our community, scan the QR code below:

https://qrco.de/LiberatedLawyerLifestyle

The client happiness coordinator can also be trained to serve as your backup intake specialist in a pinch. As you grow and have more clients, you're going to need more intake capacity, and you're certainly going to need redundancy considering humans are humans and we all get sick, take time off, or life just happens. Because your client happiness coordinator has similar skills and level of authority as your intake specialist, they can help with this role as needed.

Your client happiness coordinator can send gifts or cards to clients on the anniversary of the case you won for them. This is a nice touch that shows your clients that you still care about them, and it reminds the client of the success you achieved for them. With this yearly celebration of your winning attorney-client relationship, you'll be on their mind the next time someone they know asks for a law firm recommendation.

It's also effective to have your client happiness coordinator follow your former clients on social media and pay attention to when major life events happen. If your client has a baby, gets married, has a kid graduate, or loses a loved one, you can send a handwritten note.

You don't usually expect that from a law firm. It elevates your relationship from a purely professional one to something more personal. This exponentially increases the odds that they'll recommend you to their friends and family.

Your client happiness program can be built out to be more robust, but it's better to start with these simple actions than to not hire a client happiness coordinator at all. Over time, the program can be expanded as you add new ways to interact with current and former clients. Client retreats, anyone? Maybe someday, but let's walk before you run.

The more extensive your client happiness program is, the better your referral rate will be. But don't hold off on hiring a client happiness coordinator because you haven't developed everything fully yet. Just get started and develop the program over time.

Everything listed above can be handled virtually. Calculating a return on your client happiness coordinator is difficult, much like it's tough to measure PR. This is a feel-good position. Not only does that make it ripe for offshore, but very few client interactions occur in person these days anyway.

Finally, don't assume your client happiness coordinator can't travel for a big event once per year or your holiday party. Many of our clients have treated their staffers to wonderful trips for firm events, further cementing their loyalty.

Why Do You Need A Client Happiness Coordinator, Anyway?

There's a lot you can't control in the practice of law. You can't control the judge or the jury, for example. But you can control the client experience. Even if you get an unfair judge that gives your client a disappointing result, you can always control how you handle the client. If you want to retain clients and win referrals, the client happiness coordinator is essential.

People used to say, "Just do good work and you'll get clients." What's more accurate these days is, "Treat people great and give them a good result." That's how you'll get clients just through word-of-mouth referrals from past clients, friends and colleagues. Good news travels slowly, but it travels. Novel news spreads even faster, and having a dedicated client happiness coordinator will certainly make you novel, especially in the legal field.

If you want to retain clients and win referrals, the client happiness coordinator is essential.

When you have an effective client happiness coordinator, you no longer have to pour as much money into marketing companies that yield unreliable results. The client happiness coordinator will build a personal relationship with each client and drive them to leave reviews and refer people to you. You can increase your revenue with this organic marketing because you don't have to spend money on outbound marketing to attract each client. But doing good work and making clients feel good is a prerequisite to securing reviews and referrals.

Less than 1% of law firms have a client happiness coordinator. This is what will separate you from your competitors and get people talking about your firm. Yes, technology can help you be more efficient with client updates and outreach, but you need a human behind the tech. That will never not be true.

"It was a 'hell yes' decision."

I was thrilled when I hired my first EA through Get Staffed Up. They reviewed the job description I had, and we talked about the qualities I was looking for in the person I wanted to have work side by side with me.

We found the most incredible woman who spoke multiple languages and had not only worked for other companies but had been an entrepreneur herself. It was quickly a "hell yes" decision.

One of my first staffers worked with me directly as my Executive Assistant, but what we found is that she loved doing the marketing. That soon evolved, and later my marketing team stole her from me and she started working in that department, where she thrived. She is still with my company and has yet again elevated to another role and taken on even more responsibility.

- Kristen David, Esq., Upleveling Your Business

The Qualities of a Client Happiness Coordinator

Your Client Happiness Coordinator should be sweet and friendly like your receptionist, but should also be a bit more serious sounding, reassuring at times, and have the ability to remotely organize events. This person isn't just there to deliver the good news, they need to convince a client to take action from time to time. The client happiness coordinator should really be a people person and friendly, but doesn't need to be a 'yes' person or a consummate people pleaser.

Your client happiness coordinator's duties could include, but certainly are not limited to the following, depending on your creativity for this position:

1. Sending new client welcome kits.
2. Preparing clients for mediation by ordering their favorite types of foods and snacks.
3. Sending strategic gifts and hand written notes.
4. Organizing client and referral source appreciation events.
5. Organizing holiday parties.
6. Making current and former client outreach calls and asking satisfied clients for reviews.
7. Sending client satisfaction surveys.
8. Asking for referrals.
9. Serving as backup for your intake specialist.

Chapter Recap

The goal of a client happiness coordinator is to increase client retention, secure more referrals, and win repeat clients. With the implementation and training of a client happiness coordinator, your firm truly looks different than all the rest. Ideas on how to give better client service than other firms spew out of you daily, and you're the talk of the lawyers in town. Referrals are pouring in, being converted to clients, and your firm is doing great legal work, most of which is happening without you. A huge congratulations is in order! But before taking the next step, let's reflect on how far you've come.

24 Months to Freedom Roadmap

Seventh Hire: Client Happiness Coordinator

Cost: $2,145/month

Firm Revenues Before Hire: $47,000/month

Firm Revenues After Hire: $51,000/month

Net Gain: $1,855/month

Total Gain: $27,480/month

Hiring and Training Timetable: Months Twenty-One to Twenty-Four

For more information on how to hire a fantastic client happiness coordinator, a sample job description, weekly scorecard and more, please visit qrco.de/client-happiness-coordinator or scan this QR code now:

Part II Aggregate Recap

Because you followed our 24-month game plan, you went from around a $100,000-a-year law firm, full of stress and anxiety, to about a $600,000-a-year law firm with profits hovering around $250,000/year, full of energy and ready to take on the world.

Maybe you've invested in training to help further develop your team. Maybe you're already working with a contract paralegal and lawyer and you're ready to make your first attorney in-house hire. Maybe you've doubled down and invested in more marketing. Or maybe you've simply built a great seven-person team, and you're excited to transition into the *Visionary* role, where you start to focus primarily *on* your business instead of *in* your business.

One thing is for certain, you've taken your spouse and kids or your significant other on the vacation they've been waiting for, and you've treated yourself to some of the things you've always dreamed of. You're healthier, happier, and the sky's the limit. I know lawyers who have grown their firms from $100,000 to over $1,000,000 in 24 months. I mention this just to point out that the estimates provided in these roadmaps are actually conservative and 100% within your grasp. How quickly will you make decisions and then execute? That's up to you. It may scare you to think about growing from an $8,500 or so a month law firm to $50,000/month law firm. Don't let it. They're just numbers on a piece of paper. But the dollars will be real, as will the positive effect it will have on your family and others around you.

24 Months to Freedom Final Roadmap

Firm Revenues Before First Hire: $8,500/month; $102,000/year

Firm Revenues After Seventh Hire: $51,000/month; $612,000/year

Net Increase: $42,500/month; $510,000/year

Cost of Hires: $15,015/month; $180,180/year

Total Gain: $27,485/month; $329,820/year

Hiring and Training Timetable: Twenty-Four Months

PART III

The *Liberated Lawyer Lifestyle*

CHAPTER 10

Taking Action

"Action is the foundational key to all success."
- Pablo Picasso

Because we went an inch wide and mile deep into the seven positions your law firm needs to staff for you to thrive in Part II, it's time to talk about the Liberated Lawyer Lifestyle in the final section of this book. The part where you leave the hustle and hamster wheel for good and become the *Visionary.*

It's tempting to look around at successful lawyers and think there's something special about them and make up all kinds of other stories for why they have something that you don't. I used to do it, so I know the stories we tell ourselves. But they're not better than you. They just make different decisions than you, primarily with their time. They leverage money to get back time, and use that time to grow.

A lot of people have mental hang-ups around growth, because taking risks is scary by definition. They don't think they're ready to hire, or they tell themselves that because the thought of hiring is terrifying. Or they make up the silly rule that they need a full year's worth of someone's salary in the bank before they can hire (you know who you are!). The successful lawyers with growing firms understand the truth — if you don't hire, you won't grow. They aren't waiting for some magical day when they'll be "ready."

They're starting now because they know it's the only way out. Time is infinite, but *our* time is finite. You're as ready today as you'll ever be.

When you're in the throes of misery, it's hard to see that you could be enjoying another lifestyle in just 24 months. Thanks to the Internet, you can add major bandwidth to your team by utilizing talented people in other locations around the world who are highly competent, highly educated, and highly skilled.

You can work with these awesome people at a very low cost because the cost of living where they are is dramatically lower than in the United States. You can afford to hire a high-quality team that would crush your overhead if you tried to make all the hires locally.

It doesn't take 20 years to build a fun, profitable law firm. You can do it in 24 months.

It doesn't take 20 years to build a fun, profitable law firm that provides its owner a plethora of options for the future.

You can do it in 24 months.

And you can hire all seven members of your team that we've laid out for you for a payroll total of about under $15,000 per month. If you had to hire your whole team domestically, you would have to pay somewhere around $50,000 a month, plus the hidden 30% - 40% extra it costs in taxes, overhead and benefits to employ staff directly here in the United States. Money is no longer an excuse.

In terms of quality, when you hire internationally, if you're paying the most then you're hiring the best of the best. But you - you don't hire on price anymore, you hire on quality. And like you've heard from many of our clients in this book, the quality of staffers we find on average far exceeds what you're finding stateside for beginning level (assistant) duties.

"We're Growing and Kicking Ass!"

Our law firm was growing fast. A lot is written about growth in business with good reason. Scaling a business is incredibly difficult. Growth eats cash and finding great people takes time. All of this puts more pressure on a firm owner.

We reached out to Get Staffed Up for an executive assistant for me. **We quickly saw her work ethic and capacity and promoted her to litigation legal assistant.**

Since then we have grown immensely using both workers from Get Staffed Up - who serve in all sorts of roles from legal assistants to reception - and using domestic employees as well.

This recipe has allowed us to scale, increase the diversity of our team, and kick a lot of ass.

- Ryan McKeen, Esq., Connecticut Trial Firm, LLC

Ryan's firm, the Connecticut Trial Firm, LLC, recently secured a $100,000,000 trial verdict, the largest ever in the state of Connecticut. Ryan knows a thing or two about growing a top tier law firm. Ryan uses some of my favorite quotes - "growth eats cash" and "finding great people takes time." But when you hire smart, fast and virtual, you attack both of these challenges simultaneously.

The bottom line is that growth is made possible by adding more bandwidth to your team and getting more work done, and 90% of that comes from hiring. To handle more marketing, attract more clients, and take on more cases, you have to hire.

Sure, it costs money to hire, but you have to look at what you're going to gain. Focus on the math, not the emotion. More work out equals more revenue in. Once you have the support staff in place—the executive assistant, the receptionist, the marketing assistant, the intake specialist, the billing assistant, the legal assistant, and client happiness coordinator — you can hire attorneys and paralegals stateside and start to provide high paying jobs right in your community.

The bottom line is that growth comes from adding bandwidth to get more work done, and 90% of that comes from hiring.

As you hire attorneys and paralegals, you grow your capacity to take on even more cases and bring in more revenue. The momentum builds and your firm truly starts to operate with you needing to be at the helm. It's a beautiful thing. But you can't skip steps. Hire that rockstar staff first.

The Liberated Lawyer Lifestyle

I want to make one thing very clear - after you follow the *24 Months to Freedom* game plan, you're not ready to retire and never look back. You're not vacationing 51 weeks out of the year on your yacht or partying in the Maldives every quarter.

What we mean by *liberated* is this - when you have the team in place that we've helped you hire in the chapters above, you'll have the financial and time freedom to make choices based on *your* values, not based on fear or need. That may sound simple, but to me, that's the ultimate goal in life, to be in control of your own destiny.

Entrepreneurship isn't for everyone, and there's certainly nothing inherently wrong with being a superb lawyer or partner at a law firm who bills like crazy and crushes the work. Good for them, seriously. But you, you want to be the one in charge, making decisions - and getting to the point where, as the *Visionary*, you're *truly* making decisions based on your values, wishes, desires, wants, goals, on and on.

That is what it means to be a liberated lawyer.

With the *24 Months to Freedom* game plan, we're not taking you to the end of the entrepreneurial journey, we're removing you from the pain and misery of the hamster wheel hustle, liberating you, and taking you to the *beginning* of owning a functioning law firm with enough resources that you get to live out your dreams with whatever you decide to do next.

"We doubled revenue..."

"Force the minutiae to get out of your way."

This was the advice of one of my mentors in early 2022 as I was stressing about all of the things that I had to get done in my law firm. Our team had seven or eight people.

At this point, I already had a virtual assistant who was primarily responsible for checking my emails and handling my schedule. I had really abdicated these duties to her instead of properly training her on how they should be done.

Over the next several months, we refined our systems and processes. And as I write this towards the end of 2022, **I spend less than 15 minutes per week replying to emails.** In fact, on her performance review self-assessment, my VA Tracy wrote "Adam seems to not dislike emails as much as he did before. I remember he used to really hate them. I think that's a pretty big deal." Amen, Tracy.

The last time I went out of town, the driver was sitting in my driveway at 5am waiting to take me to the airport. As soon as I got in the car, his phone rang over the Bluetooth, and it was my VA confirming that he had actually picked me up. She, of course, booked the car for me.

I did not buy my plane tickets for that trip. I did not book my hotel. I did not book the car picking me up at my destination. All of this was handled by my virtual assistant.

As of November 19, 2022, we had doubled our 2021 revenue.

Recently, somebody asked me what the secret was to this astronomical growth. I told them: **I forced the minutiae to get out of my way.**

Now, I'm trying to plan a four-week vacation, activities with my kids over summer break, and a blow out 40th birthday party. For as much devastation as the pandemic caused, it created opportunities for my law firm in Erie, Pennsylvania (our headquarters) as we grew our team using competent and affordable staff in three countries on two continents.

- Adam Williams, Esq., Rust Belt Business Law

Want to have the biggest firm in your city, county or state? Cool. Want to never practice law again but manage the firm and turn it into the business you've always dreamed of? Awesome. Want to hire a few lawyers and then do something else? Neat.

After all, when you build your team the right way, you'll have the freedom to invest time in your family, friends, other businesses, and great vacations. You'll be making enough money to have your needs covered and have plenty of extra to do the things you want. You don't have to lie awake at night wondering when the next client will come. The firm can make money even when you're not there.

You no longer have to work with bad clients just to pay the bills. You have more than enough leads, so you can select only the best clients. The days of dealing with jerks are gone (save for the occasional client who slips through the cracks). You now have the money to create margin in your finances. You're no longer "just getting by." You can finally enjoy the lifestyle you've always hoped to have and plan for what's next.

The rest of the journey is yours. The pathway is now lit, and there is no game plan in life for what *you* want. There are roadmaps and more for building a bigger firm, coaches ready to help, conferences to attend, and masterminds to join - but that's for you to decide. You now have the *freedom* to choose, and only yourself to thank, because 24 months ago, you made a decision… and then you took action.

"We went fully virtual and hit the Law Firm 500 and Inc. 5000 Fastest Growing Companies Lists"

It was the summer of 2019. I can still very clearly recall how frustrated I felt at being unable to find top notch legal talent for my firm, Tenant Law Group, a San Francisco-based tenant rights law firm I owned and operated. We had recently experienced quite a bit of turnover, and I was in desperate need of both attorney and non-attorney staff.

At the time, we were leasing a brick and mortar office in downtown San Francisco. While the nine-person office itself was beautiful, it took me 25 minutes to commute from my home to my office and from 45 minutes to 1 hour from the office back home in the evenings when public transportation got really backed up. For anyone living outside San Francisco, the commute was, of course, even longer.

And it wasn't just the commutes that cost precious time. Whenever conventions took place at the Moscone Center, which was just a couple of blocks away, both the sidewalks and streets would fill with people, adding even more time to the commute to and from the office.

To make matters even worse, with so many firms in the Bay Area, I was competing against top-tier law firms for talent.

So, in mid-2019 to transition from brick-and-mortar to virtual.

By July 2019, we engaged GSU and interviewed a candidate named Eduardo for our Client Intake Specialist position. He was based in Mexico City, Mexico. We were very impressed and hired him.

I distinctly remember how unprepared we were for Eduardo's arrival. Although we had no real training program or even call scripts in place for him, he was smart and caught on very quickly.

Next we hired a remote receptionist. By December, we onboarded our third–my Executive Assistant.

By February 2020 we were able to eliminate our costly office expense and move all of our remaining Bay Area team to remote status.

In March we hired two more GSU Staffers.

With the help of Get Staffed Up, our firm continued to expand its team during the pandemic, adding a Case Manager, a Client Intake Specialist, and an Accounting Associate by the end of 2020.

Today, of we have a full-time team of twenty-eight, exactly half (fourteen) are current or former GSU Staffers. By the end of this month, seven Staffers will have been with the firm for over two years.

The decision to hire off site legal talent through Get Staffed Up and move to a fully virtual setup was probably the single best decision I made for this firm. To this day, I continue to realize unexpected benefits of being fully virtual with off site staff. Among them:

1. Improved Retention
2. Improved Culture
3. Better Service to Spanish-Speaking Clients
4. Expanded Geographical Coverage
5. More Time
6. More Clients
7. Improved Recruitment
8. Better for Our Bottom Line

Since onboarding our first Staffer in 2019, the firm has been repeatedly recognized for its fast growth and strong culture. **In 2019, 2020, and 2021, Law Firm 500 recognized Tenant Law Group as among the fastest growing law firms in the United States (#22, #12, and #40, respectively).**

In 2022, Inc. 5000 recognized Tenant Law Group as one of the five thousand fastest growing privately held companies in the United States. (Of the 42 law firms in the 2022 Inc. 5000 List, Tenant Law Group ranked #22 among them and #3,448 overall.) **And in 2021 and 2022, Tenant Law Group was certified as a Great Place to Work®.**

- Eric L. Toscano, Esq., Tenant Law Group

Final Thoughts

It's not easy to grow, but it is easier to run a bigger law firm with resources and backup than it is to run a firm that relies on only you or just you and a few more people. Resources give you options.

First, however, you need to take action so that 24 months from now you've been liberated from the muck. The actions are simple when broken down, but the pathway is not always easy.

There's a reason that Napoleon Hill's famous book is called *Think and Grow Rich*, not *Work and Grow Rich*.

The good news about taking action today is that you won't have to wait 24 months to see results. You'll see results immediately. When your first virtual team member begins, life becomes easier, and it gets exponentially better with every hire thereafter.

And even before you see results, you'll feel better. The moment you decide to take action, a shift happens in your brain. Your problems don't seem so burdensome anymore because you have a path forward.

You might not reach the *Influencer* stage (or wherever you're ultimately headed) for many more months or years, but as *Visionary*, you've started to see the light at the *beginning* of the tunnel and to taste the sweet freedom of what comes next. And one day you may even realize that the destination wasn't as important as the person you became along the way.

Lawyers are building great law firms by hiring virtually all around you. The question isn't whether this method works — it's whether you are going to be one of them. If you've made a real decision to take action, congratulations are in order. You're on your way off the hamster wheel and on to the Liberated Lawyer Lifestyle.

Take your first step. The freedom and ability to create the law firm of your dreams awaits you…

Bonus

Are you a "High A", action-oriented, an "Activator", or any of the other personality types who need to move right when you hear a great idea? Or, do you like a challenge and believe you can reach the LIberated Lawyer Lifestyle in less than 24 months? If so, you don't need to ruminate on the *24 Months to Freedom* game plan over the weekend or take months to piddle around, you're ready to take action now. So, for those of you ready to go, visit qrco.de/book-vip or scan this QR code and book a *Decision* Making Call with our Freedom team today.

Epilogue

Do nonfiction books have epilogues? Who cares, this one does! See that. Done is better than perfect, and be yourself.

Seriously, I'm choosing to end this book with a final section on a sincere note. I've said it before, but it bears repeating.

Show me your calendar, and I'll show you your future. No, I'm not referring to hearings or the mediation you have next week, I'm referring to all of the things you don't put on your calendar that should be there because that's how you actually spend your time - doing tiny little time-killing tasks that add up to swallow day after day, week after week.

Don't put this book down, take action!!

If your time is the most valuable resource your firm has, then why aren't you protecting it like gold and refusing to spend it on small and medium tasks easily delegated?

Some of you will wake up Monday morning, go to work and dive right into email, just like you've done for months and even years on end. Others will have someone else do their email while they bring in a new case or train someone else or get some legal work done. Both lawyers, both making very different choices about one thing - how they spend their time. Life can be really simple, and that's usually where it's most profound.

Getting more done isn't about saying yes, it's about saying no. Saying no to any person or thing that isn't a *really* great use of your time.

Saying no to unpaid consultations.

Saying no to interruptions and unscheduled phone calls.

Saying no to free legal advice.

Saying no to spending time with the lawyers not thinking like you and striving for more.

Decide to spend your time in new, focused ways, with amazing team members getting the work of the firm done for you, and watch your life change sooner rather than later.

The 80/20 Rule by Richard Koch is a short book, and yet one of the most powerful ones I've ever read. I hope *24 Months to Freedom* has been as powerful for you. That would be really cool. If not, I hope it has at least been eye-opening. I'd also settle for even a little bit helpful, because us lawyers are stubborn and wear that badge with honor, to our great detriment.

In any event, I'd seriously love to hear from you about this book. Agree with my points? Disagree? Hate the book? Love it? Enjoyed the conversational tone, or wished I had used bigger words and more than a third grade reading level because we're lawyers and should read and write like we're on law review, damnit?

Maybe you're glad you read this because you could write a much better and more profound book and if I can be successful you can too? Neat. I love human reactions. They always say more about the teller than the receiver; about who is ready to evolve and grow and who isn't. One time we sent an email newsletter out, and a female lawyer emailed us back just to say that because we spelled one measly word wrong in the email, she'd never work with us. This lady had one employee on her website, plus her office dog. I felt sorry for the dog. Oh well, can't save them all.

The fact is that some of you will take action and your business and life will dramatically improve, quickly. Some already have bigger law firms and will pass this book to a friend who needs it. Others will do nothing. Either way, I'll wake up to a great life full of endless possibilities tomorrow, with the comfort of knowing I did what I could to help you do the same. For the ones we do help, I can't wait.

Regardless of where you fall on the 'take action' spectrum, you can send me feedback at 24monthsfeedback@gmail.com. In my opinion, this would be a valuable use of your time, because of this final nugget-of-a-reason: we don't learn from experience, we learn from reflecting on our experience.

Thanks for reading.

About the Author

Brett Trembly is the founding Partner of Trembly Law Firm and Co-Founder of Get Staffed Up, Inc. 5000's #67th fastest growing business in the United States in 2022. Trembly Law represents some of the largest businesses on the east coast, as well as many small and medium-sized businesses in South Florida. Brett's passion is helping law firms and businesses grow. He lives in Miami, Florida, with his wife and three children.